To Don Cobb —
Thank you for your service to our nation.
All the best,
[signature]

The Gunpowder Prince Copyright © 2017 by Michael Archer. All Rights Reserved.

All rights reserved. No part of this book may be reproduced in any form or by any electronic or mechanical means including information storage and retrieval systems, without permission in writing from the author. The only exception is by a reviewer, who may quote short excerpts in a review.

Cover designed by Cover Designer

Cover art: Sixteenth-century Mughal Empire "Gunpowder Prince" and artillerymen. Illustration by Byam Shaw in "The Adventures of Akbar" by Flora Annie Steel (London: William Heinemann, 1913).

Michael Archer
Visit my website at www.michaelarcher.net

Printed in the United States of America

First Printing: February 2018

ISBN-97 819-8030594-1

OTHER BOOKS BY MICHAEL ARCHER

A Patch of Ground: Khe Sanh Remembered

"The best first-hand account of the battle of Khe Sanh."
— VIETNAM MAGAZINE

"An intelligent, courageous, sensitive book about a historic battle in a controversial war."
—KENNETH J CAMPBELL, Professor of International Relations, University of Delaware.

✳ ✳ ✳

The Long Goodbye: Khe Sanh Revisited

FOREWORD Magazine INDIES
Book of the Year Award 2016

"Archer has delivered a powerful sequel to A Patch of Ground, a brutally honest and impassioned work of nonfiction that takes us even deeper inside America's faltering war in Vietnam in early 1968."
—GREGG JONES, foreign correspondent, investigative journalist and Pulitzer Prize finalist, author of *Last Stand at Khe Sanh* last and *Honor in the Dust.*

"Skillfully blending history and biography, Michael Archer tells a compelling story of the Vietnam conflict and its aftermath."
— GEORGE HERRING, Alumni Professor of History Emeritus, University of Kentucky, author of *America's Longest War* and *From Colony to Superpower.*

✳ ✳ ✳

A Man of His Word: The Life and Times of Nevada Senator William J. Raggio

"Mr. Archer has rendered the people of Nevada a fascinating history lesson."
—HARRY REID, United States Senator.

"Archer's thorough research reveals his intellectual honesty and literary balance."
—DAVID HARDY, Judge, Second Judicial District-Nevada.

THE GUNPOWDER PRINCE

How Marine Corps Captain Mirza Munir Baig
Saved Khe Sanh

MICHAEL ARCHER

To those on both sides who endured the agony of Khe Sanh from April 1967 to July 1968.

"I do not think that an account of the Khe Sanh siege will be complete without an explanation of the enemy state of mind, his battle tactics and his incredible behaviour. They gave us a good fight; and, in the process, they destroyed themselves. A man [General Vo Nguyen Giap] and a force [People's Army of Vietnam], both known as past masters of guerrilla warfare, infiltration techniques and siege techniques, were finally revealed as stolid, rigid, inflexible and unbelievably foolish opponents."

—Captain Mirza Munir "Harry" Baig
December 23, 1968

CONTENTS

Acknowledgements — i

Map of the Khe Sanh Area — ii

Prologue — 1

Chapter 1   BLOODLINES — 3

Chapter 2   OUTPOST IN THE CLOUDS — 6

Chapter 3   ROAD TO DISASTER — 9

Chapter 4   EARLY INFLUENCES — 15

Chapter 5   SNOOPING IN THE DMZ — 20

Chapter 6   KHE SANH COMBAT BASE — 25

Chapter 7   A PECULIAR MARINE — 28

Chapter 8   NO ROOM FOR ERROR — 40

Chapter 9   DISPENSATIONS — 55

Chapter 10   BUTCHER BAIG — 63

Chapter 11   HARD LUCK — 74

Chapter 12   THE BUNGLED DIEN BIEN PHU — 84

Chapter 13	IMPERCEPTION	94
Chapter 14	FLEETING GLORY	99
Chapter 15	SHADOW WARRIOR	106
Chapter 16	THE GUNPOWDER PRINCE	113

Bibliography 118

Chapter Notes 122

Acknowledgments

Having worked alongside Captain Baig each night throughout the 1968 siege of Khe Sanh, I am thrilled to, at last, tell the story of this enigmatic genius who was so indispensable in saving that U.S. combat base and its defenders.

However, I would not have been able to tell the complete story, were it not for the work of Khe Sanh veteran and historian, Reverend Ray W. Stubbe. Without Ray's efforts, the sacrifices of so many young Americans and Vietnamese during the struggle for Khe Sanh would never be known. His friendship and advice over the years, and persistence in bringing Baig's early life out of the shadows, were instrumental in making this book possible.

I am also indebted to Robert DeSatte, Merle Pribbenow and Sedgwick Tourison for their copious translations of Vietnamese military records, helping me to better understand the methods and motives of the North Vietnamese Army surrounding Khe Sanh in 1967-1968.

I also wish to extend my gratitude to the following people who provided valuable information, observations, editing assistance or support over the years: Thomas Ahern, Jr., George Allen, Becky Archer, Juliette and Osman Baig, Taimur "Matt" Baig, William Bates, Timothy Castle, Bernard Cole, Robert Coolidge, Richard Donaghy, David Douglas Duncan, Mike Fishbaugh, Gary Wayne Foster, Mary Frame, Joe Haggard, Jerry Hudson, Gregg Jones, Wayne Karlin, David Lownds, Daniel Moore, Nguyen Duc Huy, Steve Orr, Raul Orozco, John Prados, Michael Reath, Kent Steen, Mark Swearengen, Robert "Doc" Topmiller, Andres Vaart, and the staff of the National Archives and Records Administration at College Park, Maryland and Vietnam Center and Archive at Texas Tech University.

My one regret is that I was unable to obtain more photographs, especially of Baig. Given the nature of his frequently clandestine counterintelligence work, I suspect, if he were "camera shy," it was by design.

Michael Archer
February 20, 2018
Reno, Nevada

MAP OF KHE SANH AREA—JANUARY 1968

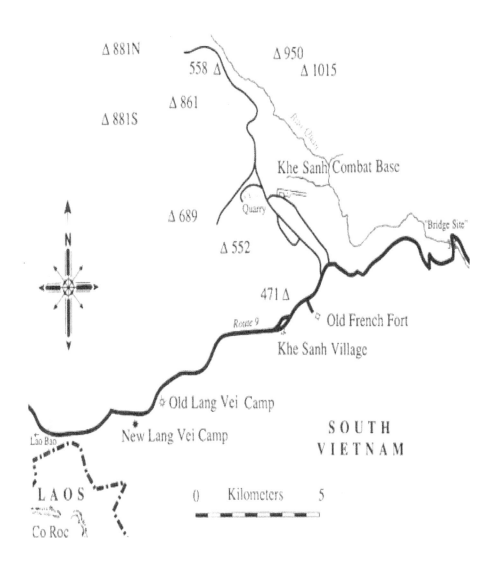

Prologue

By late-January 1968, six thousand Americans found themselves encircled by nearly thirty thousand North Vietnamese soldiers at an isolated outpost high in the Annamite Mountains of South Vietnam—called Khe Sanh. Leaders in Hanoi and Washington, seeing no end to the war, were desperate for a decisive victory that would force the other to the negotiating table. Khe Sanh was where they both decided to make that stand.

As ominous as this situation appeared for the outnumbered Marine regiment defending Khe Sanh, it was precisely what some American military leaders hoped for—luring their adversary out into the open and destroying them, by the thousands, with America's enormous advantage in air power.

The success of this gambit would rely on the courage and resolve of those beleaguered Marines—now bait in the trap—to hold on long enough to inflict such staggering attrition.

What few knew at the time was that their survival would ultimately hinge on the talent of a handful of officers responsible for predicting what this juggernaut of enemy troops, tanks and artillery, now arrayed against them, was going to do next; then expeditiously design and execute imaginative schemes to stop them—with no room for error.

Prominent among them was thirty-six-year-old, Marine Corps Captain Mirza Munir Baig, a scholarly, Cambridge-educated, Pakistani immigrant. His unique combination of classical education, years of counterintelligence work helping to develop spy networks deep into North Vietnam, and an incomparable expertise in the use of field artillery, enabled the enigmatic Baig—like a chess grandmaster—to "get into the heads" of enemy tacticians, including the legendary General Vo Nguyen Giap, and anticipate their every move.

I worked alongside this remarkable, eccentric officer over the course of the bitter ten-week siege, enduring near-constant artillery bombardment and ever-tightening enemy encirclement. Those recollections, supported by later declassified U.S. and Vietnamese military records and memoirs; leave little doubt that Captain Baig's presence at Khe Sanh was critical in averting one of the gravest military defeats in American history, saving thousands of his fellow defenders from death or captivity.

This achievement was largely the result of his early recognition that, contrary to what many still believe today, North Vietnamese activities around Khe Sanh were not an elaborate deception to distract U.S. troops away from fighting elsewhere; rather, a ruinously obsessive effort by Hanoi, sacrificing thousands of their finest soldiers, to replicate the stunning victory against the French at Dien Bien Phu sixteen years earlier.

Baig also had a personal agenda as he went about his vital work; driven by the need to erase the only stain on an otherwise illustrious family military tradition going back centuries to the Mongol conquest of the Western Himalayas. In that sense, Mirza Munir Baig had been rehearsing his entire life to step on to a stage like Khe Sanh and influence the course of history.

1
BLOODLINES

The Baig clan had its roots among the legendary mountain horsemen of the Chagatai tribe, who, in the early-sixteenth century C.E., helped create the Mughal (Mongol) Empire in what is now parts of modern-day Afghanistan, Pakistan and India. The first emperor, Babur, claimed direct descent from two of history's fiercest conquerors, Genghis Khan, a Mongol, and Taimur (or Tamerlane), a Turk. To honor his father, Umar Sheikh Mirza, Babur coined the honorific for himself of "Mirza," (meaning son of the leader, or prince); a title passed along through the centuries to those of royal heritage.

As the Mughal Empire expanded to include most of the subcontinent, its imperial forces had difficulty subduing the Muslim Sultanate of Bijapur, a task eventually requiring a fifteen-month-long siege by eighty thousand men.

Nearly three hundred years later, in 1859, British colonial forces faced the same obstinacy in their effort to subdue feisty Bijapur, when Captain Baig's great-grandfather, Mirza Imam Ali Baig, then commander of the fortress, refused to surrender. But, after weeks of siege, Ali came to realize continuing resistance was futile, and so capitulated.

Ali's son, Mirza Abbas Ali Baig, was born at this time. Family tradition has it that during the siege, his mother, while pregnant with him, bid what she believed would be a final farewell to her husband, and was smuggled out of the fort.[1] While many independence-minded Indians felt Ali's surrender to an occupying colonial army was a betrayal, young Abbas would personally benefit in life from his father's decision. The British, rather than punishing Ali for his initial resistance to them at Bijapur, commissioned him as an officer in the British Colonial Army, where he would fight with distinction during the Afghan, Sikh and Mutiny wars, eventually attaining the rank of general.

Because of Ali's station in life, his son Abbas was educated at the best schools in Bombay (present-day Mumbai). After becoming fluent in seven of the most important languages of India, he drew the attention of the British governor, who appointed the twenty-seven-year-old to serve in his office. Abbas earned a reputation for fair and competent decision making, with the *Times of India* describing him as "an able and independent representative of the Mahomedan community."[2]

In 1901, forty-two-year-old Abbas, a dashing figure with his short-cropped hair, handlebar mustache and beautifully embroidered cavalry tunic resplendent with medals, married Shaikha Aliya bin Ali, whose father was a prince in the royal family of Bahrein and her mother was the daughter of distinguished British Major General Edward Boardman. A decade later, Abbas, his wife Aliya, and their four sons, moved to London where he would become the first Indian member of the British Cabinet.

During his seven years on Whitehall Street, Abbas championed Indian causes, persuading the British Secretary of State to move forward with progressive measures, such as the partnership of India in the Commonwealth, on a footing of complete equality.

Upon Abbas Baig's retirement from the India Council in 1917, King George V bestowed upon him a knighthood of the Indian Empire and membership in the Victorian Order. Sir Abbas and Lady Baig would remain frequent visitors to Buckingham Palace, often to discuss the ancient history of the Far East with the king and Queen Mary. Abbas eventually accepted a lucrative position as finance minister for the enormously wealthy Hindu Maharaja of Baroda.

His first son, Mirza Osman Ali Baig (Marine Captain Baig's father) was born in Bombay in March 1904 and later educated at Clifton College in Bristol, England. Upon graduation, Osman entered the Royal Military College at Sandhurst by way of a personal recommendation from his father's friend—the King of England.

After receiving his commission as a second lieutenant in January 1924, Osman served with the Indian Army's Seventh Cavalry until December 1930, when he was appointed to the Indian Political Service. There, he would be responsible for the North-West Frontier Province and the strategically important Khyber Pass, along the ancient Silk Road.

While briefly back in England taking courses at Cambridge, Osman met Juliette Jamil,[3] who traced her ancestry back to the ancient Hittites of Anatolia. Juliette had been educated at the American University in Beirut and was now attending Cambridge on a scholarship personally granted by King Faud of Egypt. She and Osman married in a lavish wedding attended by several princes of India—some ranking among the wealthiest men on earth—uniquely positioning the newlyweds within rarefied social circles of world leadership from London to Delhi.

2
OUTPOST IN THE CLOUDS

Far to the east of the lavish palaces and regal society in which Osman and Juliette mingled so effortlessly in the early 1930's, amid clusters of aboriginal huts hidden deep within the misty, jungle-entwined mountains of the central Vietnam protectorate of Annam, a French coffee and fruit grower named Eugene Poilane was finally seeing modest success after a decade of cultivating his orchards.

The surrounding geography was invariably described by the occasional outside visitor as a "Garden of Eden." Monkeys, deer, feral pigs and birds flourished, and elephants roamed the river valleys; while vipers, pythons and tigers lurked in the dense mahogany groves and thickets of bamboo. The forest was abundant with wild fruit, nuts and berries; however, undergrowth in these mountains was dense and foot travel difficult due to a rugged terrain covered with vines, thorn trees and tall razor-sharp grasses.

Near Poilane's plantation, an old fort guarded part of a narrow dirt road, often barely a trail, later called National Route 9, as it passed the small village of Khe Sanh. A few miles to the west was Lao Bao, a rare gap through the largely impassable mountains that had made this road a significant trade and invasion route for millennia.

By 1940, a few additional European farmers and missionaries had settled at Khe Sanh; all dependent for labor, like Poilane, on the large, primitive Montagnard population. That year, Japanese forces arrived in Vietnam as part of an occupation plan worked out with the pro-Nazi, Vichy French government. The Japanese military's notoriously heavy-handed rule was soon felt across the country. Even the remote Khe Sanh valley was not spared the occupiers cruel discipline, with the homes of several civilians, thought to be less than loyal, pillaged and burned.

A popular guerrilla resistance movement, led by the charismatic Ho Chi Minh, began its struggle against the Japanese occupiers and would continue to fight against reinstatement of French colonial rule after the Second World War ended. Ho, who had travelled broadly, including a lengthy stay in France, recognized that, while the French might have more sophisticated weaponry at their disposal, he had unlimited human resources. If he could make the cost in casualties and francs too high, Ho knew the French would defeat themselves through political squabbling in Paris.

In early 1954, the war for independence from France came to Khe Sanh when Ho's Viet Minh forces ambushed and annihilated a large French armored group traveling along Route 9 several miles east of the village and later shelled the little settlement with mortars, wounding Eugene Poilane and killing another settler.

Four months later, at Dien Bien Phu in northern Vietnam, sixteen thousand French troops surrendered. Sapped by fifty-six days of artillery and rocket pounding, they could not resist the final, massive assault from thousands of Viet Minh soldiers. Ho Chi Minh and General Vo Nguyen Giap had stunned the world by defeating the army of a modern industrialized nation. France sued for peace.

Agreements signed during the Geneva Conference of 1954 partitioned Vietnam at the seventeenth parallel of latitude, leaving Khe Sanh within the new Republic of Vietnam, but just a few miles below the demilitarized zone (DMZ) and the new Democratic Republic of Vietnam in the north. Mandates created to form a unified Vietnamese state within two years of the agreement were ignored due to mistrust between north and south, and Cold War pressures as the United States and Soviet Union jockeyed for influence in the region.

While all parties agreed on the location of the DMZ, North Vietnam, citing a historical precedent dating to 1428 C.E., claimed a western border that was six miles farther into Laos, saying it was "intrinsically part of the Vietnamese Territory." Over the next fifteen years, they would use this as a pretext to exploit the eastern part of that neutral country as a privileged sanctuary and a supply route, later dubbed the Ho Chi Minh Trail. By late

1961, nearly a thousand northern soldiers each month were infiltrating into South Vietnam along this route.

The CIA knew the gap through the mountains at Lao Bao was a favored location along The Trail for channeling North Vietnamese Army (NVA) forces and supplies into South Vietnam. On the Fourth of July in 1962, a U.S. Special Forces team, under CIA control, moved into the abandoned fort on the eastern edge of Khe Sanh Village to monitor this infiltration and, when possible, to interdict it with bombers. An engineer unit from the south's Army of the Republic of Vietnam (ARVN) upgraded an existing dirt airstrip, on a plateau about two miles from the fort, that would later become the combat base.

In the early spring of 1964, Eugene Poilane discovered defoliant being sprayed by low-flying CIA aircraft was causing some of his trees to cease producing. He filed a claim and the Americans immediately agreed to monetary damages. Poilane would not live to see the money.

On April 20, soldiers of the indigenous National Front for the Liberation of South Vietnam, or Viet Cong (VC), stopped Poilane's Citroen along Route 9 about four miles east of Khe Sanh. They allowed his Vietnamese chauffer to flee and then, with three bullets to the chest, executed the white-bearded, seventy-six-year-old patriarch as he sat in the car.[4] The bitterness of the war had now graphically insinuated itself in the Khe Sanh area. Yet, no one then could have imagined that the tranquility of this "Eden" was about to be shattered by the bloodiest and most protracted battle of the conflict.

Four months later, the United States claimed that North Vietnam's navy attacked its vessels in international waters. This was later determined to be false, but, at the time, led Congress to approve the Gulf of Tonkin Resolution, dramatically increasing direct American participation in the war to over two hundred thousand troops.

3
ROAD TO DISASTER

About the time of Poilane's death in 1964, Army General William C. Westmoreland assumed command of all American ground forces in South Vietnam. The General believed that existing pacification programs, meant to win "the hearts and minds" of the civilian population, were taking too long, especially in the face of mounting dissatisfaction with the war back home in the United States.

Westmoreland demanded that the Marines move away from protecting larger civilian population centers and attack NVA units in their well-fortified encampments amid the jungle-clad mountains near Khe Sanh. Marine generals protested that the Khe Sanh airstrip and camp could not be defended without stationing hundreds of Marines on several hills overlooking it, and would require a major helicopter commitment because these outposts could not be supported overland.[5] They reminded Westmoreland that, from October to May, the northeast monsoon sweeping in off the South China Sea made Khe Sanh the rainiest place in Vietnam. As such, visibility for air operations and other tactical actions would be problematic for six months of the year.

Westmoreland insisted that reinforcing this isolated airfield was critical to blocking enemy movement into South Vietnam, and should be maintained as a future jumping-off point for an invasion of NVA supply dumps in Laos. More importantly, it was a perfect venue to attract thousands of communist soldiers into the open, where they could be bombed into uselessness.

The Marine generals persisted, pointing out that holding Khe Sanh would not deter the North Vietnamese from infiltrating into the south, as they had by now proven convincingly they could do without roads such as

Route 9. And, the proximity to those supply dumps within the sanctuary of nearby Laos, that Westmoreland mentioned, would give the NVA a clear tactical and geographic advantage in the battle. The North Vietnamese, they argued, could also replace soldiers faster, and with less negative political consequences at home, than could the Americans. It was, they said, "the mathematics of futility"[6] in which Hanoi would count on high American casualties to erode the national will.

General Westmoreland remained adamant, and in September 1966 the Marines acquiesced to his demand, permanently stationing units at the Khe Sanh camp. The commander of the Third Marine Division immediately warned that at Khe Sanh the NVA were going to wait until the weather closes in and then "jump on us."[7] Another, Marine Brigadier General Lowell English, a tough combat veteran of places like Guadalcanal and Iwo Jima, called Khe Sanh "a trap" and chafed at the insistence by Westmoreland to "expend absolutely unreasonable amounts of men and materiel" to defend the place. "When you're at Khe Sanh," English said, "you're not really anywhere. You could lose it and you really haven't lost a damn thing." [8]

* * *

The NVA High Command in Hanoi longed to drive the Americans out of the Khe Sanh area. Clandestine U.S. reconnaissance teams from the base were becoming increasingly effective in disrupting traffic along supply trails into the south with ambushes, the snatching of prisoners for intelligence information and, particularly, by directing air strikes on convoys, troop movements and supply dumps. This required Hanoi to permanently tie up thousands of security forces along these trails—forces that might otherwise be used more effectively elsewhere.

In May 1967, the NVA was poised to capture the combat base after positioning a thousand well-equipped soldiers in deep bunkers on hills just a few miles to the west. Marines attempting to dislodge them were caught up in two weeks of costly fighting on both sides. Marine commanders during the battle, which was later referred to as "The Hill Fights," or "The First Battle of Khe Sanh," were aware the combat base was the prize, concluding that if the NVA had successfully defended the hills for just a few more days, another two thousand soldiers waiting in Laos would have passed through them to seize the Khe Sanh base and airfield.

Throughout the summer of 1967, Marines fought bloody skirmishes with the enemy in the surrounding hills. The NVA frequently shelled the base in retaliation for these incursions, but by late August things quieted down. Marine patrols continued to roam the area throughout the rest of the summer and fall and, while the enemy remained elusive, no one doubted they were out there and planning something big.

General Westmoreland anticipated that the upcoming battle for Khe Sanh would be the greatest of the war. And, while costly in American lives, he believed it would be far more disastrous for the North Vietnamese[9] who he planned to "drown" in an unprecedented cascade of bombs, fittingly code-named "Operation Niagara." Since this remote region was relatively free of civilians, Westmoreland would have nearly unrestrained freedom to use his enormously destructive B-52 bombers around Khe Sanh.

In the waning days of 1967, Marine patrols from the combat base and hill outposts aggressively swept the area to the south and west, but found little evidence of an NVA presence. General Westmoreland suspected the Marines were intentionally avoiding the enemy to claim they were not there in the numbers he believed. In addition, a blanketing fog and steady, cold rain greatly reduced air operations, preventing the arrival of materiel necessary in strengthening bunkers to withstand the artillery, rocket and mortar attacks that everyone knew were coming.

Westmoreland viewed the Marines' inability to root out the nearby NVA, and the poor defensive posture of the base itself, yet another manifestation of their resistance to his plans. He warned his superior at the Pentagon about what he felt was the Marines' lack of "tactical professionalism"[10] and moved the Army's First Air Cavalry Division north from the central part of the country so they could quickly reinforce Khe Sanh, should the need arise.

Tension grew at the combat base as the Americans waited and watched. On January 14, 1968, a Marine reconnaissance team, patrolling on the slopes of a hill about six miles west of the combat base, discovered a battalion of enemy infantry. News of this encounter evidently distressed the NVA High Command more than it did the Americans. Their original plan had been to secretly move adequate forces and supplies into the area and then launch devastating assaults against the combat base and its outposts in early February, while the rest of the country would be preoccupied with another phase of the plan—simultaneous attacks on over one hundred cities, towns and military posts throughout South Vietnam, later known as the Tet Offensive.

However, with the Americans now tipped off to their presence so close to the combat base, and with the memory of a similar accidental discovery fresh in their minds from the previous April, when a Marine patrol foiled their plans to capture the base, the NVA High Command moved the date of the attack on Khe Sanh from its planned time in the first week in February, to January 20—just five days away. This set off frantic movements of soldiers, ammunition and food to forward staging areas. Two of these NVA regiments were returning after having fought against Marines in those Hill Fights the previous spring and "felt ready and excited about the upcoming campaign."[11]

On the night of January 20-21, 1968, the NVA launched an assault on Hill 861, a Marine outpost located two miles west of the combat base, that had been wrested from the NVA the previous April. By dawn, the Marines repulsed the attackers. At the same time, the NVA began shelling the combat base with rockets and artillery. One rocket struck the main ammunition dump, setting off most of the eleven thousand artillery and mortar shells being stored there. Those shells, in turn, rained down on other parts of the combat base causing wide-spread destruction.

The Second Battle of Khe Sanh, that General Westmoreland planned and hoped for, had begun. He was confident in his scheme to hold the combat base, and, at the same time, kill the enemy by the thousands with an unparalleled concentration of bombing and artillery.

* * *

I had arrived at Khe Sanh six weeks before, an apprehensive nineteen-year-old private first class with four weeks of training as a radio operator. I was assigned to work in the underground regimental command center on the Tactical Air Control Party, or "air team," which was responsible for informing nearby aircraft, such as close air support bombers and medevac and resupply helicopters, where our outgoing artillery fire from the base was headed, to avoid mid-air accidents.

On January 12, 1968, I was sent to the South Vietnamese District Headquarters compound in Khe Sanh village, about two miles south of the combat base, to assist the lone radio operator at a small Marine unit, called a Combined Action Platoon, advising about a hundred indigenous militia troops from the local Bru tribe of Montagnards. Nine days later, and just hours after they had attacked Hill 861, the NVA assaulted our position with hundreds of soldiers, but were unable to overrun us. We were forced to abandon the headquarters after two days of fighting and made our way back to the base.

The following night, January 23, three NVA battalions, led by seven Soviet-built tanks attacked and captured a Royal Laotian Army battalion at Ban Houie Sane near Route 9 in Laos, about ten miles directly southwest of the combat base. It was the first time in the war that NVA units had used armor in a battle; however, the Americans at first did not believe the Laotian survivors of Ban Houie Sane, incredulous that the NVA might have such a capability.

The day following my return to the combat base from the village, while I was walking to the command bunker to resume my radio duties on the air team, I had to dive for cover from an enemy artillery shell that whizzed in and exploded, leaving a small crater in the road. As I was getting up off the ground, I watched a Marine officer, who I had not seen before, emerge from the south entrance of the command bunker and, after locating the small shell crater, bent a knee to the ground and measured its dimensions with a retractable tape measure. He then searched the immediate area until he found a thumb-sized piece of shrapnel, still so hot he had to bounce it in the palm of his hand. After a brief examination of the sizzling shard, he dropped it to the ground and returned down into the command bunker.

I followed him and quickly learned that, in my absence, he had moved into a small area just adjacent to my radio desk, and was now peering over a makeshift work bench, constructed from discarded, wooden, mortar ammunition boxes, at a large map of the Khe Sanh area framed against the wall. After plotting something on the map, the man requested an artillery mission onto a target south of the base, where he reckoned that enemy gun was located.

I was amused by his peculiar Sherlock Holmes-like deductive approach to counterbattery artillery fire, made even more Holmesian when he ordered up the artillery fire mission to a nearby radio operator with a high-energy burst of British accent. I would soon learn he was Captain Mirza Munir Baig, called "Harry" by his fellow officers—but never by the enlisted men—our regiment's new target intelligence officer. It would not take me long to recognize this man's special gift for locating the enemy around us, and have no doubt that Captain Baig successfully knocked out an enemy gun team that afternoon—his first day on the job.

4
EARLY INFLUENCES

Osman and Juliette Baig's eldest child, Mirza Munir Ali[12] Baig was born January 13, 1932, on a fifty-acre summer estate that his grandfather, Sir Abbas, had built high in the verdant woodlands of the Western Ghats near Panchgani, India. Six months later, Sir Abbas traveled from London to visit his newest grandson for the first time. A few days after arriving, while giving a speech dedicating one of the buildings on his estate as a tuberculosis sanatorium in honor of his first wife and a son, who had both died from that disease, the seventy-three-year-old family patriarch collapsed from a sudden and fatal heart attack.[13]

Over the years, the Baig summer estate had hosted some of the world's most influential people. Taimur, Munir's younger brother, later recalled an afternoon when family friend Mohandas Gandhi sat on the veranda, crossed legged in his signature white, dhoti robes, while Munir chased Taimur around him with a toy gun playing "cowboys and Indians."[14]

When Britain declared war on Germany in September 1939, India mobilized. Political divisions soon came into play. The predominantly Hindu Indian National Congress, led by Gandhi, denounced Nazi Germany, but declared they would not support the fight until India was independent of Britain. Gandhi, and over sixty thousand national and local Congress leaders, were arrested. The Muslim League, however, rejected the idea of immediate independence and committed itself to working closely with the British Raj authorities, hoping it would garner British support for a later partition of the country. Throughout the war, General Osman Baig commanded Indian forces guarding the vital Khyber Pass, his family with him at his headquarters in Peshawar.

Accordingly, Munir Baig was raised in a military environment from infancy, and seemed to have absorbed every detail. In 1941, British military headquarters in London sent General Baig film of the Luftwaffe's devastating bombing of Britain, instructing him to limit viewing to government and military officials so as not to create a widespread morale problem. Young Munir was given permission to watch, and when a British officer in the audience asked about the identity of certain airplanes on the screen, the ten-year-old waited politely for a few moments, then confidently stated: "Why, Messerschmitts, of course."[15]

Four years before, Munir had already begun showing signs of this phenomenal confidence. The family was then living in Paris and a governess had taken him and Taimur to a playground in the Bois de Boulogne. Munir went off to play and subsequently returned to an empty bench where the governess was to have been waiting (she had gone off looking for him). Unflustered in his assumption that she had returned with Taimur to the hotel, six-year-old Munir walked there by himself through two miles of notorious Parisian traffic.[16]

Osman, after earning membership in the prestigious Order of the British Empire in 1942 for his distinguished service in the North-West Frontier Province, was appointed by Prime Minister Winston Churchill as the British Consul General in Portuguese India (Goa). It was here that he personally facilitated the exchange of over fifteen hundred American and Canadian civilians who had been interned in Japanese-held Asia, in return for about the same number of Japanese nationals interned in the U.S. and Latin America. It took more than a year to negotiate the deal due to security, legal, and logistical issues, and the intense animosity between the U.S. and Japanese governments. Munir was enthralled by the uniqueness and complexity of the matter and enormously proud of his father's patience and negotiating skills.

During the war years, Munir and Taimur received the best education possible, always in the British tradition their father so admired. In May 1945, soon after the German surrender, but with Japan still very much in the war, Osman enrolled thirteen-year-old Munir, and ten-year-old Taimur at his prep school alma mater, Clifton.

That summer, a thousand children and mothers, and another thousand British soldiers, embarked on a troop ship from Goa to England. Munir's mother remained bedridden with seasickness until the vessel steered into the calmer waters of the Red Sea, then was finally able to go on deck.

There, to her delight, a ship's officer exclaimed: "Thank God for your son, Munir!" He went on to explain that crew members had been frustrated early in the voyage with the rowdy behavior of several "English brats." Munir took charge, intentionally misleading the children into believing that he had seen a Japanese submarine trailing the ship, probably looking for an opportunity to sink it. He then organized the youngsters into two shifts, with a promise of a prize to the one who spotted the enemy sub first. Order was soon restored.[17]

After graduating from Clifton, Munir continued to Trinity College at Cambridge University, pursuing a degree in law and joining his mother in London on weekends to enjoy the city's excellent operas, ballets, theaters and restaurants.

During this time, the partition of India was underway. While most of the subcontinent would remain predominantly Hindu, large sections in the northwest and northeast would form into the new Muslim nation of Pakistan. Although Gandhi hoped to avoid partition, Muslim leaders promoted it as a way of preserving their rights. The result was a cataclysmic mass relocation of nearly fourteen million people, with Hindus, Sikhs and others moving from what was now Pakistan to India, and Muslims moving from India to Pakistan. It is believed that as many as a million people were killed in the upheaval, the result of rioting and retributive genocide between ethnic and religious groups passing through each other in opposite directions.

Violence and political assassination marred Pakistan's newly gained independence. Although Osman had declared Pakistani citizenship, he sensed it would take years to develop into the kind of nation in which his western-educated sons could safely survive and possibly lead by dint of their heritage. Juliette, even more fearful for her children's safety—and without advising her husband—registered the boys for permanent residency status in the United States. Taimur, born in Quetta, now part of Pakistan, had little difficulty acquiring that status; but Munir, having been born in India, was denied due to an extraordinarily restrictive immigration quota from that country at the time.

In 1946, Osman was appointed to the post of counsellor at Pakistan's embassy in the United States. Refined and well connected, he and Juliette easily fit into Washington diplomatic society. Three years later, he transferred to the consulate in Canada; and, in 1953, Osman, now High Commissioner, opened Pakistan's embassy in Ottawa. His sons left Cambridge to join their parents. Taimur would soon enter Harvard, and Munir took up studies at prestigious McGill University in Montreal, earning a master's degree in business administration.

Eventually, Osman came to agree with his wife's concern about Munir's tenuous immigration status, and was able to use his diplomatic connections to obtain for his son the status of permanent resident alien in the United States as a Pakistani national.

In 1955, Munir's uncle Selim Jamil, an executive with the national retailer Sears, Roebuck & Company, recommended him for a junior executive position at the company's headquarters in Chicago. As a resident of Paris in 1917, Selim had worked with the American army, assisting Acting Quartermaster General, Robert Wood. Brigadier General Wood later become CEO of Sears and, remembering Selim's knack for supplying the U.S. army in France with local produce and commodities, brought him into the company.

In 1942, President Franklin Roosevelt inquired privately of General Wood whether he knew of anyone with the contacts, linguistic ability and knowledge of the Middle East to help clandestinely channel food and other supplies to the Soviet Union, via Turkey. Wood recommended Selim, who had his roots in Lebanon, and he was soon dispatched to Beirut where he successfully carried out that secret mission for the remainder of the war.

Young Munir immediately disliked the monotonous and restrained nature of corporate culture, and his Uncle's tales of international intrigue during the Second World War—at the personal behest of President Roosevelt—did nothing to diminish his yearning for a more adventurous life.

A few years earlier, Munir had received a crushing blow to his boyhood dreams of glory. His curriculum at Clifton was designed to prepare him for admission to the Royal Military College at Sandhurst; but when the time came for him to enroll, relations between the governments of Pakistan and Great Britain were strained. Osman's high diplomatic status within

Pakistan's government now voided the "legacy" admission he felt would come from his father's alumnus status.

Osman knew his son's aspirations and how disappointed he was, writing him in a letter: "If you still want to pursue a military career, the only real military organization left in the world is the United States Marine Corps."[18] His admiration for the Corps was fueled by a close friendship with Felix De Weldon. In 1945, Congress commissioned Austrian-born, artist De Weldon, to create a sculpture as the centerpiece for a new Marine Corps War Memorial, based on the famous photograph depicting six Marines raising the American flag on Iwo Jima

On their summer break from Clifton in 1947, Munir and Taimur sailed aboard the Queen Mary from Southampton to New York City. Days later, the boys joined their parents for dinner at De Weldon's Washington townhouse. The Marine Corps Memorial sculpture was then still only a small prototype, and fifteen-year-old Munir spent much of the evening in the artist's studio gazing at it. "Munir," his mother later said, "was enchanted with the model."[19]

In late 1956, two years after De Weldon's one hundred-ton bronze statue was finally unveiled in Arlington, Virginia, Osman sought him out to assist his son in becoming a Marine officer. De Weldon took Munir directly to the Commandant of the Marine Corps, General Randolph "Mc.C" Pate, who advised the young man that, despite his exceptional education and prestigious family background, federal law required that all military officers be U.S. citizens—though this rule did not apply to enlisted ranks.

Undeterred by his Sandhurst rejection, and now barred from officer training in the United States, Munir remained conscious of a grander personal destiny and was determined to have a military career. In February 1957, he enlisted as a private in "the only real military organization left in the world." Before boarding a train at Union Station in Washington, D.C. for his trip to Marine Corps boot camp at Parris Island, South Carolina, Munir kissed his mother goodbye saying, "Don't fret, mama, I shall make you proud of me."

5
SNOOPING IN THE DMZ

At twenty-five, Munir Baig was considerably older than the average Marine recruit. Yet, he not only survived the rigors of boot camp, but was named as his platoon's "Honor Man." He continued to excel in the Corps, earning the rank of sergeant within two years and was awarded Meritorious Mast for superior performance as a legal clerk at Marine Barracks, Brooklyn, New York. He reenlisted in early 1959, and was assigned to one of the Navy's newest aircraft carriers, the *USS Independence*, operating off the coast of Virginia. Candidates for such Marine guard detachments aboard capital ships in the U.S. fleet were selected from the among the most able, "squared away," in the Corps.

Osman Baig was now Secretary General of the Central Treaty Organization (CENTO), a mutual defense and economic cooperation pact among Iraq, Iran, Turkey and Pakistan, with United Kingdom and U.S. participation. In early October 1959, he requested, through the U.S. State Department, that his son be flown to Washington D.C. to act as his aide during a week-long CENTO Conference. The next day Sergeant Baig was catapulted from the deck of the *Independence* to join his father.

The savvy Osman would have to employ all his diplomatic skills to hold the organization together after the sudden withdrawal by Iraq damaged its credibility. It was a stimulating week for Munir, whetting his appetite for a broader life experience. As a reward for his son's effort, Osman used his connections in the United Kingdom to have Munir awarded the Coronation Ribbon by the Queen of England, though Sergeant Baig would not, by regulation, be permitted to display it on his American Marine Corps uniform.

In early 1960, Sergeant Baig was assigned as an instructor at the Marine Corps Sea Indoctrination Course, known as "Sea School," located at Norfolk

Naval Shipyard, Portsmouth, Virginia. In March of that year, he became a citizen of the United States. With this final impediment now behind him, Baig accepted a commission as an officer. The selection board recommendation described him as "an outstanding Marine."[20]

Just three days before his training began in May 1960, Baig married twenty-year-old Diane de Rochefort, daughter of French Count Nicholas de Rochefort. Diane had attended school in Barcelona, Spain and then the University of Madrid, before immigrating to America in 1959. The ceremony was held beneath the towering dome and celebrated mosaics of the Catholic Cathedral of Saint Matthew in Washington, D.C. Baig, surrounded by his Marine Corps buddies, wore an immaculate dress white uniform with sword. The reception at the Fort Lesley J. McNair Officers Club was attended by five hundred guests.

The environment at Officer Candidates School, in nearby Quantico, Virginia, was different than Baig had known as an enlisted man. Unlike boot camp, where recruits were trained to think as a group and look out for one another, Marine officer training was more individually competitive. At five feet, seven inches, and one hundred twenty-five pounds, the twenty-eight-year-old Baig was slighter and considerably older than most of his fellow candidates. Despite this, many in his training company took a genuine liking to this uncommon Marine, nicknaming him "Harry" and "hauling him up and down" the grueling trails of the Virginia countryside.[21]

Upon completion of Officer Candidates School, Second Lieutenant Baig moved on to the next phase of his training, a twenty-six-week-long course called The Basic School, also at Quantico. Once this basic training was completed, Baig received orders for Camp Lejeune in North Carolina, where, in May 1961, Diane gave birth to their daughter, Cecile Juliette.

* * *

The following year, Second Lieutenant Baig was assigned to the U.S. Army Artillery and Missile School at Fort Sill, Oklahoma for training as an artillery officer and returned to Camp Lejeune as commander of a 155mm self-propelled gun battery. In 1963, he was selected to attend the Intelligence Research Officer Course at Fort Holabird, Maryland.

His father-in-law, Count Nicholas, appears to have recruited his new son-in-law into the intelligence business. Nicholas was born in 1902 in St. Petersburg, Russia where his father represented French financial interests. As a member of one of France's oldest families, with ancestor Guy de Rochefort earning fame during the First Crusade in 1095, Nicholas served as a captain in the French Army during the Second World War. Captured by German forces, Nicholas soon tricked his captors into releasing him from a POW camp near Lubeck, Germany by feigning an illness. He joined Allied forces after the Normandy invasion, serving with the First French Armored Division.

After the war, de Rochefort, who spoke five languages, edited a periodical in Morocco before beginning a lecture tour in the United States in 1949. Five years later, he renounced his French citizenship and title and became a U.S. citizen. As an expert in psychological warfare, Nicholas served on the faculty of American University in Georgetown and as a research analyst at the Library of Congress for the Agency for International Development,[22] which, during the 1960s and 1970s, was a cover organization for CIA officers abroad.[23]

Now a first lieutenant and newly trained intelligence officer, Baig was assigned to the Third Counterintelligence Team, Third Marine Division, arriving in South Vietnam in September 1963 to serve with the Ninth Marine Expeditionary Brigade (Marine combat units did not arrive in Vietnam until 1965). With only an indigenous jeep driver/translator, Baig traveled hundreds of miles along bumpy, dirt roads throughout the northern part of the country and along the DMZ, with no protection, other than his sidearm. There, he studied terrain features, NVA infiltration routes and the rhythms of their movements. During his travels, he acquainted himself with the civilian populations, cultivated local informants and helped set up a network of spies that eventually extended deep into North Vietnam:

> I was the Division G-2 [Intelligence staff] clandestine, intelligence coordinator for military intelligence agencies

in the Division TAOR [tactical area of responsibility]. The 15th Marine Counterintelligence Team and U.S. Army intelligence units had established collection nets far across the Ben Hai River. These nets had penetrated several NVA headquarters and other organizations. 24

Baig also interrogated enemy prisoners captured by the South Vietnamese Army to determine the strength and immediate intentions of NVA forces infiltrating south to help the VC. Former Marine Major Bill Bates, a friend who visited with Baig several times while the two were in Vietnam, recalled long conversations that left Bates with the distinct impression "some of Harry's techniques in interrogating were not so pretty," and that he may have been actively involved in early "kill teams" to remove VC sympathizers.25

In November 1964, Baig was assigned to Marine Corps Air Station, El Toro, California as a counterintelligence officer. There, he used his expertise to train Marine helicopter and bomber pilots in squadrons that would soon be operating along the DMZ.

He was promoted to captain in April 1965 and returned to South Vietnam in the summer of 1966, just in time to participate as an artillery officer during Operation Hastings in which twelve thousand U.S. Marines and ARVN attempted to push approximately ten thousand NVA back across the DMZ. In late 1966, Captain Baig was sent to Amphibious Warfare School in Quantico, then returned to South Vietnam and was assigned as executive officer with the First 155mm Self-Propelled Gun Battery, Third Marine Division, and later, as commanding officer. Bill Bates visited Baig at his battery near Phu Bai. "I was at his compound one night," Bates recalled, "when VC sappers penetrated into the ammo dump and blew it up. We had quite a firework show for several hours, but Harry took it in stride. He was one of the best, most professional Marine officers I ever met."26

After thirty days leave back in the U.S., Captain Baig returned to his battery in September 1967, but was soon transferred to serve as an intelligence officer at Third Marine Division headquarters in Dong Ha. During this time, he urged his friend and fellow intelligence officer, Major

Bob Coolidge, to arrange a meeting with the commanding officer of the Division, Brigadier General Louis Metzger.

With great poise, a short, curved, wide-bladed khukri sword in a scabbard on his hip,[27] and stomping a boot occasionally for emphasis in the British military tradition, Baig presented an intelligence briefing in meticulous detail.

Drawing on Marine Corps tactics employed earlier in the century in places like Haiti and The Philippines, Baig proposed to the general that a mobile guerrilla force composed of Marine noncommissioned officers be sent to live off the land, roaming the Ho Chi Minh Trail for intelligence information and interdicting NVA reinforcements and supply convoys. After Baig departed the meeting, the general looked at Coolidge and remarked: "Is he for real?"

While General Metzger may have been put off by the captain's grandiose style, he was likely impressed with Baig's tactical inventiveness and clear assessment of problems dealing with NVA infiltration. What Metzger knew, that Baig evidently did not at the time, was a clandestine mobile force, much as he had envisioned, was already operating in Laos. The Military Assistance Command, Vietnam–Special Operations Group, later renamed Studies and Observations Group (SOG), a highly classified, multi-service special operations unit, was routinely carrying out reconnaissance missions along the Ho Chi Minh Trail, kidnapping prisoners for interrogation, calling in air strikes on NVA troops and supplies, emplacing electronic sensors along infiltration routes both in the western DMZ and in southeastern Laos, and engaging in psychological warfare operations. The primary jumping off point for SOG operations was a compound adjacent to the Marine base at Khe Sanh.

These activities were so secret they were managed directly from a special office deep within the Pentagon, and only after assuring the State Department that operatives would carry no identification that might jeopardize the appearance that the United States was honoring Laotian neutrality as a signatory of the Geneva Accords of 1962. The SOG accomplished much of what Baig hoped such a unit would, especially in forcing Hanoi to divert thousands of troops to rear security missions along the Trail.

6
KHE SANH COMBAT BASE

The Khe Sanh Combat Base command center bunker was constructed in October 1965 to house ammunition, but was converted after the enemy first began shelling the place three months later. Set out in a north-to-south rectangle about seventy-five feet in length, most of the bunker consisted of several small rooms and two larger rooms, located off a single narrow corridor. The larger rooms were each about twenty feet square and directly connected by two window-like openings through the adjoining wall. The interior was unfinished cast-in-place concrete with several large roof beams supported by vertical wooden posts, twelve-inch square. The seven-foot-high ceilings had, over the years, become cluttered with drooping electrical and telephone wires.

Once the siege began, NVA gunners concentrated, in earnest, on knocking out the command bunker. When one of their larger shells exploded close by, the impact would shake equipment from wall pegs, and cups would dance off tabletops on to the floor. A rain of dust and loose gravel would descend from the crumbling concrete ceiling, and, mixed with the ever-present cigarette and cigar smoke already in the room (the only ventilation being portable electric fans) would create a harsh fog that momentarily obscured objects even a few feet away.

One of these large rooms was occupied by Khe Sanh's commanding officer, Colonel David Lownds, and his regimental staff, including several radio operators. There, officers would follow the tactical situation on a large map that took up much of one wall.

Leading up to the siege, the Marines' supply problems extended beyond acquiring necessary bunker building materials, to almost every facet of life. At one point it was discovered that Colonel Lownds did not have a map of the Khe Sanh sector providing enough detail to adequately carry out the mission (standard tactical maps at the time used 1:50,000 scale). Because there was nothing better available to him, a Navy Construction Battalion "Seabee," skilled in technical drawing, offered to painstakingly draft, in free hand on large pieces of butcher's paper, a map at a scale of 1:10,000. Consequently, the map used by the base commander to orchestrate the greatest pitched battle of the war, was not created by a professionally trained cartographer, but by a construction battalion enlisted man.[28]

The other large room was used as the Fire Support Coordination Center (FSCC). Activity in this room was always highest at night, when the enemy liked to move about and would most likely attempt an attack. During a typical twelve-hour night watch, a tightly assembled group of men did their work. This included me and my fellow radio operator, Lance Corporal Raul Orozco, working with Captain Richard Donaghy, the regimental air liaison officer with expertise in helicopters, and Marine Captain John Fitzsimmons, who specialized in close air support bombing. Captain Kent Steen, and his immediate superior, Lieutenant Colonel John Hennelly, with the First Battalion, Thirteenth Marines, represented the local artillery contingent. Assisting them, were four radio operators using landline telephones to communicate with the fire direction component and artillery batteries spread across the base. They were supervised by Gunnery Sergeant Leon Risch, a salty Korean War combat veteran.

In addition, U.S. Army Captain Mark Swearengen, liaison for the long-range guns located up to a dozen miles to the east at the Rockpile and Camp Carroll, and Naval Gunfire Liaison Officer, Lieutenant (Junior Grade) Bernard Cole; shared a tiny makeshift desk. The regimental intelligence "shop," occupied by Major Jerry Hudson, was in a small foyer leading up a few steps from the FSCC room. The newest arrivals, Captain Baig and his assistant, Marine Staff Sergeant Robert Bolsey, had squeezed into a space between our air team desk and the doorway.

Captain Swearengen, who also had just arrived at Khe Sanh, later recalled his first meeting with Captain Steen in the cramped FSCC room. With notebook in hand, pencil poised, Swearengen anxiously awaited a detailed briefing on the disposition of enemy forces. Steen, the gifted, twenty-six-year-old Floridian responsible for prioritizing enemy targets now tightly encircling the combat base, paused for a few moments, not knowing where to begin. Finally, exhaling a short sigh of exasperation, Steen swept his hand in a broad circle over the map and said simply: "They're everywhere."[29]

He was not exaggerating. The NVA now had about twenty-seven thousand troops in position. Of them, nine thousand were infantry riflemen, half of whom were armed with assault rifles, the remainder carrying older weapons, and nearly four hundred with rocket-propelled grenade launchers. Crew-served weapons included more than one thousand five hundred light- and heavy-machine guns, forty recoilless rifles and one hundred eighty mortar tubes.[30] This force also included five artillery regiments, three antiaircraft gun regiments, four tank companies, five engineer battalions, a communications battalion and a few local VC-led militia units. [31]

This was one of the largest and best-supported attack forces ever fielded by the Vietnamese, and, as it tightened its noose around the scattered and out-numbered Americans at Khe Sanh, seemed invincible. Most of us would have rather been somewhere else, but not Captain Baig. His long-awaited moment in history had finally arrived.

7
A PECULIAR MARINE

Bespectacled, scholarly, with an aristocratic manner and accent, Captain Baig seemed out of place in the grunginess and muck of the combat base and the coarseness and youthful bluster of the troops there. That, combined with the unusual, nonregulation accoutrement he wore, including a short, wide-bladed, inwardly curved, khukri sword in a scabbard on his hip; and a Boy Scout pack he had purchased from Sears as a nod to his former, and only, civilian employer, left many of us concerned that Baig's over-refined flair indicated a lack of the toughness required to defeat the enemy around us.

We would not have to wait long to learn why this peculiar character had been placed in our midst. His dual expertise in counterintelligence and artillery, accompanied by a steely sense of purpose and the instincts of a jungle predator, equipped Baig intellectually and temperamentally for the life-or-death challenges he was about to face.

His first test was to winnow through a staggering amount of, often dissonant, intelligence information to ascertain the enemy's intentions and tactics. Up until the siege began, the Khe Sanh area had been a playground for a variety of American intelligence gathering units and mysterious individuals. In addition to SOG, there were CIA-sponsored civilian agents and members of the Defense Department Joint Technical Advisory Detachment, who made deeper penetration into Laos.

Others, like the U.S. Army's Counterintelligence Team, the South Vietnamese National Police (and their own counterintelligence units) and United States Special Forces teams stationed at Lang Vei, five miles from the combat base, were all out collecting information on NVA infiltration into South Vietnam along the Ho Chi Minh Trail. These sources ranged in complexity from local Montagnards hiding alongside a road with simple clicker-like radio devices designed to count soldiers and vehicles as they passed; to SOG teams with state-of-the-art, night-vision glasses and electronic detection equipment.

However, all this information was going directly to their own distant headquarters, while those at the nearby Khe Sanh base remained uninformed and in constant peril, except when those various headquarters would eventually pass along old, incomplete and processed intelligence, which, by then, was almost always useless.

Consequently, Marines at the combat base were forced to rely on their own close-in patrols from local infantry and reconnaissance teams, and a small unit working with the indigenous militia in nearby Khe Sanh village. Starting in October 1967, Colonel Lownds, who had personally familiarized himself with much of the local terrain around the base (often trekking out with just a radio operator, or occasionally alone), began receiving alarming reports that the CIA's helicopter-borne "people-sniffers," sensitive to the odor of human sweat and urine, were making hundreds of detections close by, in areas that had been considered uninhabited jungle. Soon, hundreds of sorties were being flown over Khe Sanh, some with radio direction finders.

High-altitude saturation bombing was deemed the best way to deal with such threats. Air Force Boeing B-52 Stratofortress bombers, originally designed as a major component of the United States' nuclear warfare capability, would now be used as conventional bombers over South Vietnam. Code named "Arc Light," a typical mission consisted of two sets of three bombers arriving ten minutes apart and passing over a target area approximately one-mile long, by one-half-mile wide. Each plane dropped thirty tons of high-explosives from an altitude of over thirty thousand feet, with almost no warning to those in the target area. As such, they were much feared by the NVA and often cited by defectors as the primary reason for that decision.

The Khe Sanh command center was now receiving information from photo reconnaissance missions, that included flights by highly classified U-2 aircraft; aerial infrared technology; side-looking airborne radar (which helped detect the movement of vehicles); and records from the CIA's National Photographic Interpretation Center in Washington.

It was clear that the number of NVA soldiers encircling Khe Sanh base was swelling rapidly—but by how much, and where were they hiding? Major Hudson recalled the absurdity of spending months frustrated at obtaining virtually no intelligence information—and now suddenly having far more than he could absorb.

"It was about that time that Harry Baig and Bob Coolidge arrived," Hudson said. "We began to put some direction and order to this mass of information and tried to keep Colonel Lownds advised so he could make timely decisions and prioritize his decision-making process."[32] Coolidge would work days as the target intelligence officer and Baig worked nights. Soon they, along with Hudson, were feverishly collating and evaluating thousands of bits of information on a daily and nightly basis.

Sir Abbas Ali Baig and son Osman, circa 1910. (*Baig family*)

Shaikha Aliya bin Ali, Lady Baig, circa 1910. (*Baig family*)

Vo Nguyen Giap (left) and Ho Chi Minh, 1942.
(National Archives and Records Administration)

Wedding reception in May 1960, Fort McNair Officers Club, District of Columbia. (L-R) Diane de Rochefort Baig, Second Lieutenant Munir Baig, his parents, Osman and Juliette. *(Baig family)*

The Gunpowder Prince

The First Battle of Khe Sanh, or Hill Fights, May 1967. After U.S. Marines dislodged a thousand North Vietnamese soldiers preparing to capture Khe Sanh, they would then permanently occupy key hilltop outposts overlooking the combat base. (*National Archives and Records Administration*)

General William C. Westmoreland and President Lyndon B. Johnson meeting in Saigon two months before the Tet Offensive. (*National Archives and Records Administration*)

Aerial view of roughly the center of Khe Sanh Combat Base, February 1968. Airstrip is seen in lower half. The regimental command bunker is located at center of photo, in the smudged-appearing area near an intersection of the main street and the loop street. The Marine's southern perimeter trench line is in the upper part of the photo, just past where the base's structures end. Just above that, is a horizontal road which was held by our NVA besiegers. Their zigzag trench lines are barely seen near the very top. (*Marine Observation Squadron VMO-6, National Archives and Records Administration*)

U.S. Air Force B-52s dropping bombs over South Vietnam. Three of the six aircraft that comprised every Arc Light mission.
(National Archives and Records Administration)

Hand-delivered top secret seismic sensor being deployed near Khe Sanh in early 1968. *(National Archives and Records Administration)*

North Vietnamese Army artillery piece firing on Khe Sanh Combat Base in 1968. *(People's Army of Vietnam)*

U.S. Marine howitzer firing from the outpost on Hill 881 South in 1968. *(National Archives and Records Administration)*

One of several U.S. cargo planes destroyed by NVA antiaircraft fire while attempting to land at Khe Sanh Combat Base, February 1968. *(Joe Haggard)*

In January 1968, when discussing Khe Sanh, President Johnson told his Joint Chiefs of Staff, "I don't want another damn Dien Bien Phu." Here he frets over a sand-table model of Khe Sanh in the situation room of the White House. *(National Archives and Records Administration)*

Author facing away (at left) and Raul "Oz" Orozco at the Air team desk in the FSCC room of the regimental command bunker, January 1968. (*Raul Orozco*)

Staff Sergeant Robert Bolsey, Captain Baig's assistant (at left) plotting target information on Baig's map. At right, is the author reading a book. The photo quality suffers from water damage to the original negative. (*Michael Reath*)

Regimental Air Liaison Officer Captain Richard Donaghy (left) and Navy Lieutenant Bernard Cole, "Commander, Naval Forces, Khe Sanh," in the FSCC room of the regimental command bunker. (*Michael Reath*)

Colonel David Lownds, ultimately responsible for the decisions made at Khe Sanh, including his trust in Captain Baig's unusual methods, sits in a lawn chair with his signature cigar, contemplating the fate of his command. (*Author's photo*)

8
NO ROOM FOR ERROR

While Baig's aptitude for using defectors, spies and radio intercept intelligence to their maximum destructive effect was truly remarkable; perhaps his greatest accomplishment was the ability to teach himself an entirely new source of information—a top secret, highly complex, air-supported, anti-infiltration barrier system. Developed at a cost of nearly a billion dollars, the technology was so secret that few in the U.S. military, and no one in the South Vietnamese government, even knew about it.

Captain Baig's prior knowledge of the system was limited and theoretical. In the summer of 1966 he was invited to a secretive meeting in Santa Barbara, California of the Institute for Defense Analyses, Jason Division. The Jasons were a group of world-class scientists who met each summer since 1960 to tackle problems that the Defense Department could not solve. At this meeting, they were asked to study the practicability of the anti-infiltration barrier system[33] and Baig's invitation stemmed from his expertise in NVA infiltration habits acquired during his counterintelligence work along the DMZ in 1963.[34]

Eighteen months after that Santa Barbara meeting, Baig, and his fellow targeting officers, now in the midst of battle, somehow would have to become experts on this complex and untested system. Keenly aware that failure to master the process quickly and fully would result in disaster, added enormous pressure on the group—and on Baig in particular. Few times before in U.S. military history had a junior officer faced such a daunting responsibility with almost no room for mistakes. Baig later equated the experience with that of children being tossed into a river and having "to learn to swim on our own."[35]

The system used two types of sensors deployed around Khe Sanh to collect information about enemy movements. One, the Air-Delivered Seismic Intrusion Detector, had been developed from existing technology used by the oil industry for underground mapping. These seismic devices reported vibrations made from passing troops or vehicles, and were placed in carefully plotted "strings" along trails or roadways. The other type of sensor was an acoustic device called Acoubouys, a variation of U.S. Navy anti-submarine equipment. It was designed to float down on parachutes, also placed in carefully plotted patterns, into treetops and blend in with the foliage. A sensitive onboard microphone would then be able to pick up sounds of movement, including conversations. To detect troops who moved too quietly, the area around the acoustic sensors often was seeded from the air with small anti-personnel "gravel" mines that exploded when stepped on, activating the sensors.

Sensors would transmit information to specially equipped U.S. Air Force EC-121 aircraft circling overhead around-the-clock, which was then relayed to the high-security Infiltration Surveillance Center (ISC) located at an airbase near Nakhon Phanom, Thailand, where it was fed into several IBM 360-40 mainframe computers. Once analyzed, the ISC issued a 'Spotlight' report to the intelligence unit at Khe Sanh. The process usually took thirty to fifty minutes. "I was extremely aggravated by the delay," Baig said, "because the enemy had by then departed and no action could be taken."[36] A secure direct circuit from the ISC soon was provided, vastly improving the time it took Baig to receive the target information.

At first, it was difficult to determine what had activated a sensor. Rather than the enemy, the activity might have been passing elephants, tigers or even monkeys, who, Baig commented wryly, "were suddenly wondering what they had done to deserve an artillery barrage." Often, explosions from our own bombs and artillery, even some distance away, would activate a sensor.

Spotlight reports did not differentiate between seismic or acoustic activations. Baig repeatedly, though unsuccessfully, requested specific information about the makeup of a string of sensors and whether the two types were interspersed. This was further complicated by the fact that the enormous loads of bombs dropping day and night around the base from B-52s, often changed the appearance of the terrain so drastically that low-flying delivery aircraft would sometimes inadvertently drop new sensors (the devices had a battery life of only thirty days) in the wrong areas, providing Baig with wildly inaccurate locations.

As awe-inspiring as this billion-dollar, top secret, intelligence gathering system was in theory, it was useless unless the data could be interpreted in the context of the NVA's intentions and methods. Baig later wrote that he had based his planning, procedures and doctrines in fighting the NVA not only on those disciplines he learned in the military, but on the writings of General Vo Nguyen Giap. Giap, like Baig, was a student of eighteenth-century siege warfare and First World War artillery tactics and techniques. Because both men were fluent in French, it gave Baig access to many of the same archaic volumes that Giap had read.

This is what made Captain Baig's contribution so critical to the survival of Khe Sanh. What would prove to be more important than his expertise in counterintelligence and artillery, was his lifelong penchant for classical scholarship and his genius in applying conventional warfare's most sophisticated technology to an adversary who insisted on employing antiquated siege tactics and artillery techniques. "I found this information invaluable at Khe Sanh," Baig said.[37]

He brought four basic "assumptions" with him to Khe Sanh: (1) the enemy would follow a master plan which had been promulgated from a headquarters, not on the field; (2) the NVA commander in the field at Khe Sanh could not and would not alter the battle plan to any significant degree, even if new conditions arose; (3) the modus operandi was predictable and the general concept determinable once the opening moves were known; and (4) the plan encompassed classic siege tactics as practiced and studied by General Giap during the siege of another isolated Khe Sanh-like fortification fourteen years earlier at Dien Bien Phu. Since that 1954 battle, Giap had made only one modification to that plan.

During September 1967, after attempting to subdue Con Thien, another U.S. Marine combat base near the DMZ, Giap first realized the Americans were routinely maintaining a significant buffer between U.S. and South Vietnamese forces, and areas being targeted by B-52 bombers.

He was correct. Early in the war, the Americans instituted rules to ensure the safety of their own and allied forces, by setting minimum distances, which varied with the type of ordnance being used. A B-52 strike was required to be no closer than three thousand meters (about two miles), due to fear of concussive effects from the hundreds of high explosive bombs detonating at once.

Consequently, by the time the NVA moved again on Khe Sanh in early 1968, Giap had slightly altered the master plan he had used to achieve victory in 1954, by having his advance assault troops quickly assemble within that two-mile buffer zone around Khe Sanh base and its outposts. Baig immediately requested the CIA furnish him with aerial photos of Viet Minh entrenching activity around Dien Bien Phu.

* * *

Baig originally, but incorrectly, assumed the Spotlight map coordinates showed the locations of enemy troops or vehicles that had triggered the sensor, and so he quickly fired on it. From subsequent conversations with ISC staff, he learned the Spotlight coordinates were not the location of the *target*, but of the *sensor*, whose actual position could only be determined within a two-hundred-meter probability of error. As such, Baig later said, "those coordinates ceased to be attractive as targets." His frustration led him to the innovative concept of evaluating Spotlight reports not in terms of targets—but in patterns of movement.

Baig knew the NVA relied on mobility to keep their adversaries guessing; occupying an artillery, anti-aircraft gun, bivouac or headquarters position for a short time; moving from one to another; often, completing a circuit back to original position. Consequently, his focus now shifted from where the enemy *is*, to where they were *going to be*.

He and his colleagues painstakingly collated information from sensors, intercepted enemy radio transmissions, Montagnard spies out in the countryside, daily aerial photos and analysis of incoming shell craters and shrapnel fragments. The "total picture" that emerged involved locations of reserve forces and routes of reinforcement and retreat. These targets were often more significant than the NVA assault forces in their trenches and bunkers right up against the combat base and outposts—because Baig already knew where they were.

Instead, he focused his attention on who was supporting those troops, and how they were doing it. Soon, a clearly identifiable pattern emerged. From their assault forces in front of the combat base and outposts, extending miles south and west into rear support areas, the enemy was constructing a series of bunker complexes, anti-aircraft and mortar positions, ammunition dumps and logistic areas; as well as fuel dumps and maintenance parks for their vehicles along the main approaches to Khe Sanh.

Of this, Baig later wrote:

> Where we began to get a lot of nocturnal sensor activity in any unexpected area, we would examine that area in the morning to see if there were any signs of construction. Frequently, we did find such signs. So rather than making the mistake of disturbing the enemy troops who were causing the sensors…we decided to wait until they got to their destination and became concentrated. Then we would knock out the whole thing with one blow.

His decision to change tactics by not immediately targeting the area of a sensor activation was quickly criticized not only by those at the ISC, but also by the senior officer onboard the EC-121 airborne command center flying overhead, whose radio call sign was "Moonbeam."

Baig recalled one acrimonious conversation on the radio that he and Lieutenant Colonel Hennelly had with that aircraft:

> We were asked by someone named Moonbeam to state why we did not fire at certain targets. We told them that we didn't consider that target to be more important than some other target. He couldn't see our argument at all. I finally told him that if he wanted to run the war he could come join us. [38]

Obviously aware of the precarious position we were in on the ground at the time, the offer was met with radio silence. "After that," Baig said, "he [Moonbeam] did not make any more comments on the subject."

Baig's special understanding of his adversary's history and tactics allowed him to grasp what Moonbeam and those in the distant computer center did not; that unless the NVA succeeded in completing certain stages of development—and in a certain order—they would not be successful. Baig:

> He [the enemy] built himself a colossal complex of bunkers in certain portions of the Khe Sanh perimeter that we could see exactly what he intended. We knew his timetable by the progress of each development. Sensors...led us to the new enemy installations and the new support areas and new antiaircraft positions he was building. When he brought in the 37mm antiaircraft guns, he dug for two days in getting them established and, with sensors we found them immediately. [39]

He saw details in such predictabilities that few others did. For example, the NVA designed their bunker complexes, supply and ammunition dumps, etc., using the same rigid formula in layout, dimensions and spacing between locations that they had been using for decades, what Baig termed "doctrinal position area engineering." Therefore, it only required him to identify a small portion of a position to destroy the rest of it, as well as other positions in proximity to it—often sight unseen!

Nevertheless, there were some surprising and frustrating exceptions. Truck and armored vehicle traffic was still moving along Route 9 with impunity after dark. When these vehicles heard U.S. aircraft overhead they would simply turn off their headlights and stop moving, making them indiscernible. Accordingly, Baig needed aircraft equipped with side-looking, radar to locate them. But, because they were required to fly at extremely low altitudes to be effective, it curtailed American artillery fire into the area for fear of hitting the aircraft. "So, we were balancing the use of such aircraft on one hand," Baig said, "against denial of artillery on the other hand, and frequently we'd have to tell the aircraft to go home. But, even with the subsequent artillery fire, we could not completely block the road traffic."[40]

Also, North Vietnamese soldiers quickly figured out the patterns of air-delivered sensors and became increasingly effective in finding them. Once they detected the location of a sensor, they immediately began to search out others in the string and destroy, or reposition, them. Simply changing the course of their movements to avoid passing by the sensors was not always an option given the rugged, terrain around the combat base, limiting the number of roads and trails. Consequently, while the NVA negated the effects of numerous sensors in this way, so many of them were sown that a majority survived.

Transmissions from acoustic sensors located by the NVA were particularly revealing, because the excited conversations of those who found them were clearly audible. In one instance, a long, profanity-laced excoriation of the device was followed by a woman's plea: "Let me shoot it. It's my time to shoot!"[41]

* * *

By late-January 1968, military and political leaders in Washington were growing increasingly apprehensive about what was unfolding at Khe Sanh. Despite the enormous amount of American firepower unleashed around the combat base, the enemy seemed stronger than ever. President Johnson convened a meeting in the White House on January 29, polling each member of the Joint Chiefs of Staff about whether the U.S. should make a stand at Khe Sanh. All agreed they should, although by that time the prospect of quickly and safely removing the thousands of Americans already there seemed an impossibility.

Johnson was obsessed with avoiding another Dien Bien Phu, and installed a sand table terrain model of Khe Sanh in the Situation Room of the White House to follow the events. The president understood the consequences of that long-ago battle at Dien Bien Phu better than most. As Senate Minority Leader in 1954, he opposed providing U.S. military assistance to save the beleaguered French Union forces trapped there. This included a suggestion by some in the military to use tactical nuclear weapons.

The use of such nuclear artillery, under a plan code-named "Operation Fracture Jaw," was also being considered in the 1968 defense of Khe Sanh. Those of us at the combat base during the siege heard rumors that special gun sights had been secretly delivered to our artillery battalion for such a mission. Like most rumors, they proved to be untrue; but remained a source of anxiety among those of us who felt that nothing good could come from such an experiment.

The Jasons, at their March 1967 meeting in Santa Barbara, had produced a top-secret report to the Pentagon advising on the possible use of tactical nuclear weapons in Vietnam.[42] It is not clear whether Captain Baig provided input on this issue; but, as someone whose expert advice had been solicited by the Jasons just six months before, it would not have been a surprise. His expertise not only encompassed a unique familiarity with the terrain and patterns of NVA movement, but also his skill as an artillery officer capable of firing nuclear-tipped artillery shells.

In their report, the Jasons presented a significant downside to American use of nuclear weapons in Vietnam in the prospect that such an escalation could prompt retaliation against the U.S. military's large and stationary bases there—perfect targets for Soviet-supplied nuclear weaponry.[43]

* * *

American intelligence analysts were convinced that the NVA headquarters for the entire Khe Sanh campaign was located near the tiny village of Sat (also spelled "Sar" or "Sap") Lit in Laos, about twenty-five miles northwest of the combat base, in an area previously known for its unusual geologic spires and deep natural caves. On January 30, 1968, the U.S. Air Force hammered Sat Lit with scores of B-52 bombers. Airborne observers counted nearly one hundred secondary explosions, indicating the target area was heavily invested by enemy forces. The wealth of NVA radio transmission intercepts from that site, which had helped lead the Americans there, was completely silenced. It was the largest bombing mission up to that point in the war, but because it had taken place in "neutral" Laos, this spectacular military success was kept secret from the press.

The next day General Westmoreland sent a classified memorandum to the U.S. Ambassador in Laos speculating whether General Giap may have been in that now shattered headquarters complex. Like Westmoreland, those of us then at Khe Sanh were hoping that the fifty-six-year-old Giap, who was rumored to be personally commanding the Khe Sanh front, had been caught in that attack. Giap remained a national hero after Dien Bien Phu, but what few outside Hanoi knew was that his influence had been marginalized months earlier.

By July 1967, the ascendant militant faction, led by Party First Secretary Le Duan, was concerned that the relentless American bombing of the north, coupled with recent, costly fighting in the hills around Khe Sanh between U.S. Marines and crack NVA battalions, would soon drive a consensus in the Politburo to sue for a negotiated peace. To prevent that, he ordered the arrest of hundreds of moderates, military officers and intelligentsia, pushing the venerable Ho Chi Minh and General Giap aside in what was later called the Revisionist Anti-Party Affair. While it was a common belief by those in the western world that the struggle for national liberation was fought by a unified leadership and patriotic volunteers from both the north and south. Lien-Hang T. Nguyen, a Columbia University historian of the Vietnam War, with particular expertise on the workings of the Communist Party leadership in Hanoi, points out that: "In reality, Le Duan constructed a national security state that devoted all of its resources to war and labeled any resistance to its policies as treason."[44]

With moderates now out of the way, Le Duan, and Army Chief of Staff General Van Tien Dung, set in motion the plan for a broad conventional military offensive that would strike hundreds of targets in South Vietnam. They believed the south was ripe for change and would erupt in a popular uprising at the sight of communist forces in the streets.

While a launch date for the campaign against Khe Sanh had to be moved up to January 20 after NVA preparations there were accidently discovered by the Marines, the nationwide offensive was still planned to begin ten days later, on January 31, the first feast day of Tet, during a holiday ceasefire agreed upon with the Americans and South Vietnamese government.

Years later, information would surface that then-Defense Minister Giap had traveled to Eastern Europe in September 1967, ostensibly for medical treatment. Many felt Giap's absence was due to his opposition to Le Duan's plan for the Tet offensive. Giap believed the U.S. was poised to attack North Vietnam by land and sea and that his forces should be kept closer to home to repel the invasion. He also guessed that, in conjunction with the invasion, Americans would launch from Khe Sanh Combat Base to destroy NVA supply depots along the Ho Chi Minh Trail in Laos.[45]

Giap did not return to Hanoi until January 31, just in time to join the NVA High Command in agonizing over the devastating security failure that led to the destruction of their headquarters at Sat Lit. Soon after that bombing, Giap arrived in the Khe Sanh area of operations to help stabilize that situation and boost morale, but then departed, according to one of his subordinate generals, "not only because we feared for his safety—but also because he had urgent duties directing the fighting everywhere."[46]

The destruction of the campaign headquarters at Sat Lit resulted in a widespread breakdown in communications across the Khe Sanh front. Two days after surviving the bombing of his headquarters, the commander of the Khe Sanh campaign, General Tran Quy Hai, now at his new makeshift operations center several miles northeast of Khe Sanh, received a landline telephone call from Army Chief of Staff General Dung. The High Command had made the decision to stick to the initial plan and timetable for Khe

Sanh and ordered him to press the attack more vigorously. This spurred Hai to action, and early on February 4 his troops moved into position to launch attacks against two hill outposts west of the combat base, Hill 881 South and Hill 861 Alpha, a newly fortified knoll adjacent to Hill 861. Dozens of sensors began activating.

This occurred at a time before Baig had figured out how to use the sensor information effectively, and so he decided to resist the temptation to infer anything because, as he later wrote, "it would be folly to become erudite in one's ignorance."[47] Therefore, he believed what the sensors purported to say; that fifteen hundred to two thousand troops had reached a point about two miles northwest of Hill 881 South.

He initially thought this to be a convoy of resupply porters, rather than assault forces, and reacted by attacking each sensor target as it became known. But, by night fall, he had modified his belief, and was now envisioning an enemy infantry regiment ready to attack Hill 881 South. Coolidge and Hudson concurred that an attack in the thick fog now shrouding that hill was imminent.

Baig's understanding of NVA tactical doctrine led him to anticipate correctly that the attacking force would move to its assault position in echelons, make a last-minute reconnaissance, and then attack in waves. If this were a regiment, the force would be dispersed in regimental column, battalions on line, one behind the other. Knowing the size of the force and its probable rate-of-march in that dark, foggy terrain (about two kilometers an hour), Baig identified a point they likely had reached since activation of the last sensor.

He quickly devised a target box south of that hill and commenced his first barrage at 3 a.m. on February 5, pouring in continuous fire from the Khe Sanh base, and more distant artillery batteries at the Rockpile and Camp Carroll, for about thirty minutes. The enemy threat to Hill 881 South was now broken, and acoustic sensors recorded the anguished screams of some of the many hundreds of NVA soldiers fleeing down the hillside in panic. Baig's devastating artillery fire plan spared the Marine defenders on 881 South from heavy casualties, perhaps even enemy capture of the hill.

However, just as Baig and the other FSCC officers began to breathe a little easier, two NVA battalions, consisting of nearly a thousand soldiers, moved unnoticed to the northeast side of Hill 861 Alpha. While one battalion quickly attacked the Marine lines and penetrated the fortification, the second battalion stayed down the hill in reserve. Since no sensor strings had been placed on the approaches to this newly built fortification, Baig used his uncanny comprehension of the adversary's military history to surmise the location of "all the possible assemble/reserve areas at the base of the hill" and destroyed the reserve battalion who, he later wrote, "met a revolting fate, attended to by one hour of shelling and air strikes."[48]

Captain Mark Swearengen's distant 175mm guns now created a "wall of steel" which moved slowly from the area where the NVA reserves had been trapped, up the slopes until it reached a point two hundred meters from the Marine's barbed wire. The defenders slowly gained the advantage and pushed the attackers back off the hill and into that murderous rolling barrage.

When it was over, Captain Baig was furious with himself for not identifying that the NVA plan was to attack *both* hills, and self-mockingly shouldered responsibility in a later report:

> When the latter [Hill 861 Alpha] was attacked two hours later, I, the Target Officer, an alleged expert on NVA doctrine, was caught flatfooted... once more, Marine NCOs [non-commissioned officers] and other ranks made up for the mistakes of the alleged brains of, and on, the staff, as they have done throughout our history.[49]

* * *

The day after the failed February 5 attacks on Hill 861 Alpha and Hill 881 South, the NVA's 304th Division, Ninth Regiment, about fifteen hundred troops, was ordered to capture the Khe Sanh Combat Base, and be prepared to ambush hundreds of reinforcements they expected would soon be arriving by helicopter. As the night march moved forward in a nearly mile-long column beside a meandering stream, the Second Battalion was completely engulfed in an Arc Light Baig had targeted.

The First and Third Battalions, marching behind them, were not hit in the initial strike, but when they rushed forward to assist the casualties, a second wave of B-52s arrived overhead and hundreds of bombs exploded among them. "Flames and smoke filled the air," the stunned Third Battalion commander later wrote. "Dead and wounded soldiers lay strewn through the trees and bushes on both sides of the stream."[50]

The regiment sustained hundreds, perhaps over one thousand casualties. While the exact number is unknown, records in Hanoi later indicated that over two hundred were killed in the Second Battalion alone, and large quantities of weapons and equipment destroyed. The loss of so many of their comrades had an immediate impact on the morale of the survivors. "A number of soldiers deserted, or shot themselves so they could be taken to the rear," a regimental history later recorded, "but others wanted to directly attack the Americans in order to get revenge for their unit." The Second Battalion, quickly rebuilding with replacements, would retain the honor of being the "the primary assault battalion during the campaign to liberate Khe Sanh." [51]

Within hours of this devastating loss, another NVA battalion, using Soviet-built tanks, flamethrowers and supporting heavy artillery fire from nearby Laos, captured the U.S. Army Special Forces camp at Lang Vei. Captain William Dabney was commanding the Marines on Hill 881 South, three miles north of Lang Vei, but was in no position to help. He later summed up the hopelessness of the Lang Vei predicament: "[They] were not going to hold off twenty thousand men who have artillery and tanks! They should never have been there." For Colonel Lownds, Dabney said, "it was a foregone conclusion there was going to be a tragedy. I believe he saw it coming, but he lacked the authority to do anything." [52]

Indeed, Lang Vei's usefulness in the interdiction of NVA vehicular traffic along Route 9 was quickly becoming a non-issue, because they were building a significant truck road just a few miles south of, and parallel to, that highway. Ironically, it was by way of that new road that the NVA had gotten their tanks into position to launch the surprise attack on the camp.

The fighting at Lang Vei was costly for both sides. Indigenous forces suffered three hundred nine killed, sixty-four wounded, and one hundred twenty-two captured. Of the twenty-four American defenders, seven were killed in action and three taken prisoner. The remaining U.S. survivors, almost all of whom were wounded, were rescued later that day by a helicopter-borne U.S. Army reaction force. The battle marked the first use of tanks by the NVA within South Vietnam. They later claimed to have lost ninety soldiers killed and two hundred twenty wounded.

No sooner had Lang Vei fallen, when a reinforced Marine platoon guarding a knoll just a few hundred meters west of the combat base came under intense mortar attack followed by a broad infantry assault. The defenders were quickly overrun. Of the sixty-four Americans, twenty-four died and another twenty-nine were wounded.

These were incredibly desperate days for the defenders of Khe Sanh. With the fall of the District Headquarters in Khe Sanh village and the Lang Vei Special Forces camp, and ferocious attacks on nearby hills, it now seemed the momentum generated by these two NVA divisions, with their tanks and artillery, might not be stopped. Soon an unmistakable sense of doom was evident on the faces and in the conversations of almost everyone. By the end of that first week in February, it was like the cold, gloomy Khe Sanh fog had crept down into the corridors of the command center.

This sense of despair was not merely due to the NVA's success in rolling up outposts in preparation for a mass attack on the combat base, or that the entire country of South Vietnam was now reeling from the Tet Offensive. Two weeks before, on January 21, the same day of the initial attacks on Khe Sanh, North Korean commandos were stopped while attempting to assassinate South Korean President Park Chung Hee. Two days later, North Korean naval vessels and MIG Jets attacked the *USS Pueblo* as it gathered intelligence information off their coast. One American was killed and several were wounded. The ship and eighty-two surviving crew members were taken captive.

The risk of retaliation by South Korean and American forces remained high. Given the coincidental nature of these attacks with what was happening at Khe Sanh, and the close diplomatic relationship between

Pyongyang and Hanoi, it immediately raised the question of whether these events were coordinated between the two governments, possibly to distract attention from one, or the other.

The U.S. was already pitted in Vietnam against the sixth largest army in the world, and might now soon be fighting North Korea's 350,000-person military. In between, and bordering both countries, was the People's Republic of China, hostile to the United States and its allies. Though China was then in the destabilizing throes of a Maoist purge called The Great Proletarian Cultural Revolution, it could be dangerously unpredictable, and might send hundreds of thousands of its troops into the fray, as it had done in Korea in 1950.[53]

If U.S. aircraft and troops were to be diverted from Southeast Asia to fight a new war to protect South Korea, the Pentagon would be forced to make tough decisions on how to use their remaining resources in South Vietnam most effectively. Those of us hunkered down at isolated Khe Sanh were grimly aware of our expendability in such a scenario.

About that time, Captain Baig created several transparent overlays for his map, each covered with rectangular grids representing a space about one mile long by one-half mile wide. Each grid was marked with a distinct identification number that could be used to quickly request a devastating Arc Light on that specific area.

One night in early February, I commented to him that our command center was in the center of one of those numbered grids, to which he replied: "That's correct Bru,[54] just in case this place should abruptly change ownership." He then chuckled softly at the dark irony of his having to finish our besiegers' job for them.

Over the succeeding years I have been unable to find a satisfactory answer as to whether, having been pre-targeted for such a bombing, the Pentagon would have given final approval? And, if so, had they fully vetted all potential consequences of that decision? As an example, if we had been overrun by the enemy in a replication of Dien Bien Phu, there would have been many hundreds of American captives. Would these lives have been a price the commander-in-chief was prepared to pay to increase the enemy body count and deprive North Vietnam—now with a stupendous propaganda victory in hand—an additional windfall in captured U.S. arms and equipment?

We had all come to rely on Captain Baig, like some chess grand master, to have worked out in his mind the details of every possible scenario. Yet, this did not seem to me to be the way he envisioned an end to a life so fated with lofty historical purpose—a shattered, unidentifiable corpse entombed with two dozen others in the rubble of the command center after a self-inflicted bombing.

9
DISPENSATIONS

To better organize targets and prepare them for destruction, Captain Baig was assisted by Staff Sergeant Robert Bolsey. Each night, finely sharpened pencils in hand, the two men would laboriously annotate and update hundreds of index cards with bits of new intelligence information. Each card represented a single, one thousand-meter-square map grid. Soon the cards were filled with a wide variety of possible targets. These included rocket-launching sites; artillery, automatic weapons, mortar and anti-aircraft weapons positions; fortified areas with bunkers and trenches; camp and assembly areas; logistic dumps; and truck and tracked vehicle parks.

I worked within a few feet of Bolsey each night and found him to be pleasant and unpretentious, though not giving up too much information about himself. I have rarely met a person who so completely subordinated his own ego to the job at hand.

In the early days of the siege, I would often join him at dawn climbing a ladder to the top of the watchtower located at the south entrance to the command center. At first light, Bolsey would peer through binoculars into the dissolving ground fog to catch a glimpse of NVA soldiers feverishly digging trench lines toward us. One morning in early February, he was scanning the terrain to the south and, to his surprise, saw an NVA officer with binoculars looking back at him from a window in the main house of the Poilane coffee plantation about a mile away. Later that morning, the house was bombed to rubble.

As enemy artillery shells inched increasingly closer to the command center, someone suggested that the watchtower was being used by them as an aiming reference point; after which, Colonel Lownds ordered the tower pulled down.

Because of the meticulous collection and collation of information through their card filing system, Baig and Bolsey eventually produced over three thousand separate targets within a nine-mile radius of Khe Sanh. Baig later said:

> We had far more known and confirmed targets than we could possibly use. Mortar and artillery positions, of which the former was not worth counting and the latter exceeded one hundred sixty separate sites, were bombed and shelled nightly in patterns of fire corresponding to NVA doctrinal position area engineering to destroy the unseen battery ammunition dumps.[55]

One evening, an awestruck Major Hudson summed up the feelings of the rest of us in the room when he blurted out: "Harry, you have a head like a computer!"

* * *

Requests for B-52 Arc Light missions were to be submitted at least fifteen hours prior to the drop, although occasionally bombers on the way to South Vietnam, from distant air bases on Guam, Okinawa and in Thailand, could be diverted to "emergency" targets. But, Arc Lights could never be as responsive or flexible as the use of smaller, tactical aircraft and artillery. Ideas were brainstormed among officers in the FSCC about how to combine the strengths of both. Baig's study of NVA tendencies, especially in their larger unit maneuvers, identified predictabilities making them easy prey for what became the team's imaginative "time-on-target" schemes of concentrated artillery fire in tandem with radar-controlled bombing. The resulting techniques were dubbed Mini-Arc Light and Micro-Arc Light.

The Mini-Arc Light could be put into effect in about forty-five minutes against suspected enemy assembly areas, or likely routes of movement, delivering fifty-six bombs from radar-controlled aircraft, and two hundred thirty artillery and large mortar shells, all within an area five hundred meters by one thousand meters at almost the same moment. Enemy soldiers caught in the zone had no chance.

When more immediate firepower was required, a Micro-Arc Light could be executed in ten minutes. The area size was reduced to about five hundred square meters, with twelve to sixteen bombs and one hundred thirty rounds of artillery and mortar arriving simultaneously. On an average night, three to four Minis, and six to eight Micros were executed near the Khe Sanh Combat Base. When designing these missions, Baig recalled with morbid humor: "Our motto was 'Be Generous.'"[56]

* * *

One of my duties on the air team was to monitor the results of the radar-controlled bombing missions and record the pilot's assessment of bomb damage, such as the number of secondary explosions he observed while still above the target.

At first, it was both exciting and reassuring to hear how extensive the damage was that we were inflicting on the enemy from the air. But after listening to hundreds of these sorties, I became adroit at knowing when some of the pilots were incorrect, or embellishing the level of destruction.

If, for example, I knew the target was a platoon-size NVA unit on the move, rather than trucks or an enemy supply point (the pilots, flying at fifteen thousand feet, did not know the nature of the targets), and they responded that there had been numerous, large secondary explosions, I usually treated that with some skepticism. Although, if the bomber had been part of a Mini- or Micro-Arc Light, the simultaneous artillery shells exploding the target area could be mistaken for secondary explosions.

Weather permitting, an aerial inspection of the bombed site would be attempted as soon as possible. The NVA, however, were meticulous in hiding their damage and dead. Eventually, we concluded that bomb damage assessment by the pilots was less than scientific, and so collection of this information became less important to us.

There were often so many aircraft circling above Khe Sanh that we had to send some back without dropping their bombs, usually due to fuel considerations. A bomb-laden fighter-bomber coming from Da Nang or Chu Lai would have only about twelve minutes on station over Khe Sanh before having to return to base.

To try and squeeze in as many sorties as he could, Captain Baig would frequently give me a Spotlight report on recent enemy movements and let me plot their new probable location on my map. I would then telephone the Marine Air Support Radar Team at the other end of the base with my map coordinates and they would guide the next bomber in the queue over that target. This was heady stuff for a nineteen-year old private first class, and I would always listen more intently to these bombing runs on my radio and—human nature being what it is—was more likely to accept the pilots' estimates of bomb damage on the missions I had plotted.

Another of my air team responsibilities was to retrieve aerial reconnaissance photos of enemy positions encircling us. Each morning at sunrise, a single-engine Cessna, possibly attached to CIA-operated Air America, would fly low over the base's main east-west road and drop a canvass satchel containing aerial photos out of the plane's door. I always volunteered for this duty of standing out on the road and popping a smoke grenade to mark the drop spot, despite the risk, because the bag usually included goodies for me from the pilot: a can of cola, some candy bars and occasionally a copy of *Playboy* magazine. As soon as the satchel hit the ground, I would grab it and race back underground just ahead of NVA gunners homing in on my smoke.

These eight by ten-inch, black-and-white, glossy photos typically showed the progress of NVA trench lines as they crept closer to us each night. Exact copies were often shown to President Johnson, as he fretted about Khe Sanh in the Situation Room of the White House. It occurred to me later that if the carbonated drink in that satchel had exploded on impact, it might have ruined these photos so vital to our defense. I wondered how it would be explained to the president why the commander of perilously besieged Khe Sanh base did not get his copies that day.

To reinforce that progress was being made at Khe Sanh, General Westmoreland's staff inundated the commander-in-chief with data. Their daily reports included a variety of claims about "confirmed" and "probable" enemy killed, as well as an obsession with Bomb Damage Assessment, in which they even tallied Yards of Trenchline Destroyed (YTD). In the Khe Sanh FSCC room, we often wondered about the value of the YTD; spawning an amusing and ongoing "philosophical" debate about whether a bomb landing in a trench destroyed it—or enlarged it.

* * *

Crowded into the Khe Sanh command bunker FSCC room was a diverse staff from three different military branches, composed of infantry, intelligence, artillery and aviation officers, all with their own view on how best to save the combat base from falling to the NVA. Add to that, the strain of constant shelling, ground attacks and deplorable living conditions, and it was easy to see how the group might have become divided and quarrelsome. Yet, they quickly developed into a harmonious team, encouraging and accepting new ideas and displaying great humor and camaraderie despite the grim circumstances.

Much of the credit for this must be given to Lieutenant Colonel John Hennelly, who sat each night, calm and dignified, on a stool in a corner of the room.

Captain Baig agreed:

> Lieutenant Colonel Hennelly kept us all together and judiciously prevented us from running amok in the FSCC with outrageous propositions. In emergencies his intellect enabled to him to maintain control of nine batteries firing continuously on shifting targets and one radar-controlled

air strike every ten minutes. No one else in the FSCC could have done so.[57]

Initially, it had not been easy for Hennelly and Lownds to overlook Captain Baig's brashness and eccentricities, or offer their total confidence in his judgment. Baig recognized this. Credit for saving the combat base, he later said, must go to Colonel Lownds who had the final word on all decisions. Lownds had fought and bled as a junior officer during the Second World War in such infamous places as Saipan and Iwo Jima, but was a progressive-enough thinker to trust in Captain Baig's theory that traditional Marine Corps tactics and doctrines, so effective earlier in the twentieth century, must be tweaked at Khe Sanh to fight against an enemy "who chose to put his faith and fortune in the usages of the eighteenth [century]."[58]

Catholic Chaplain Father Walt Driscoll visited the FSCC room regularly and once remarked that the place:

> Seemed so rational, so under control, despite all the turmoil and chaos and despite the fact the enemy had been advancing their trenchlines toward us on the south side of the base to a point where they were just three hundred yards from the FSCC room.[59]

The proximity of an NVA battalion just a few minutes' walk away kept most of us on edge, but Captain Swearengen recalled that "when Baig talked about being surrounded by thousands of enemy troops he would just bubble with enthusiasm! It would scare the daylights out of most people, but he was enthused about it!"[60]

A few weeks earlier, when Swearengen had first arrived at the base, he noticed the apprehensive mood in the FSCC room, later recalling there appeared to be no apparent recognition yet "of the magnitude of the threat building up around us." Then a few days later, "Harry shows up with his British accent and khukri knife at his side and spoke as though he were there to single-handedly save Khe Sanh. I thought, 'Is this guy crazy?'"

Swearengen immediately realized this was exactly the kind of enthusiasm and positivity they needed right then: "It didn't take long to realize Harry was not really out to accomplish everything by himself. He was one heck of a team player and always asked for advice and opinions from others."[61]

The presence of our Naval Gunfire Officer, Lieutenant Cole, was a constant source of amusement because we were so far out of the range of any American war vessel. Cole played along with our good-natured teasing, such as acting disappointed when his "unemployment check" failed to arrive in the mail. On his little makeshift desk, there soon appeared an official-looking placard announcing: "Lieutenant Bernard D. Cole, Commander, Naval Forces, Khe Sanh." Despite having virtually nothing to do in his field of expertise, he proved to be an enormous help to Baig in sorting out the endless stream of data pouring in each night about enemy movement around us. Cole greatly admired Baig and his positive outlook:

> New ideas, jokes, gibes, prognostications, criticisms/praise of the C-ration meal he had just opened ('Aha! I have biscuits!' the British term for cookies), interplay with others in the bunker, both enlisted and officer—he seemed always to be in motion physically and active mentally.[62]

Our C-rations were a regular joke in the FSCC room because Captain Baig, despite his lean frame, had a prodigious appetite. When supplies dwindled, he ate things others would not, like the much-maligned Ham and Lima Beans. A radio operator once asked, "Captain Baig, I thought Muslims couldn't eat pork?" Without missing a beat (or a bite) Baig replied with a wry smile: "That is true, but when we kill the infidel, Allah will give us dispensations." Everyone laughed, until another radio operator interrupted, saying: "I don't know what we're laughing about, to Captain Baig—we're all infidels!" It was true that Baig entertainingly referred to those of us around him, and the NVA, as "infidels;" but it was clear from his punishing attacks on the latter just which infidels would be providing such dispensations.

Despite his ready wit, Baig could be passionately intolerant of ineptitude and always spoke his mind. I do recall him lashing out impatiently at Staff Sergeant Bolsey on occasion, which Bolsey never seemed to take personally. Major Hudson, recalls:

> Harry was very, very professional, very intense. Somebody around him who was anything less than that, he'd drive them nuts. He'd jump up and yell, 'Incompetence! I cannot stand incompetence!' That's the way he was. He had very, very high standards for himself, and he expected all those that worked with him to be the same. [63]

One evening while he was reviewing an aerial reconnaissance photograph, Baig thought he recognized truck tire tracks converging on a certain location about two and a half miles south-east of the combat base. I was looking over his shoulder at the time, but my untrained eye could not identify anything resembling that. Later that night, as bombers approached that target, I went outside to watch. The little hill erupted in secondary explosions and would burn and explode for hours. Baig had found a major ammunition dump in less than three weeks. It had probably taken the NVA months to secretly stock it.

I returned underground and told Captain Baig about the pyrotechnics. He and Captain Steen decided to go up and see for themselves. As they stood watching, a large mortar shell, probably a "short round" from one of our own batteries, but one that had traveled far enough to be fully armed, bounced in front of Baig and rolled to a stop at his feet. Miraculously, it did not go off. Steen was astonished by Baig's composure and asked him if he were frightened, to which he quietly replied: 'No, it is not my time."[64]

"Harry," Lieutenant Cole later wrote, "was absolutely fearless."[65]

10
BUTCHER BAIG

After the loss of hundreds of their Ninth Regiment's troops to an Arc Light strike as it moved to attack Khe Sanh base on February 6, the NVA High Command temporarily adopted a passive approach, changing their focus from assault to encirclement. Some of their units were sent from the Khe Sanh area to help in the fighting at Hué about sixty miles to the southeast. The NVA still kept the combat base tightly surrounded in preparation for the final big push to capture it, feeling safe in their knowledge that the rules of engagement prevented B-52 bombers from striking within three thousand meters of American forces.

The regiment's Second Battalion, eager for revenge, while still frantically rebuilding their ranks, excavated an elaborate system of trenches and bunkers opposite the Marine lines. The forwardmost of these extended to within just a few hundred meters of the regimental command bunker, where Baig was busy plying his trade to stop them. At times, he could feel the shuddering groundwave of bombs he was directing on these nearby positions as they inched toward the base, adding clear-cut immediacy to his work and enormous pressure on him to make each decision a correct one—or face prompt, and potentially fatal, consequences.

As they dug ever closer to the Khe Sanh perimeter, a deputy political officer from the NVA's 304th Division headquarters visited the besiegers, telling them that, because they were so close to the combat base, the Americans "would become fearful and demoralized."[66] Far from being demoralized, the Marines at the combat base were straining for an opportunity to run them off.

On February 25, the day the battle of Hué officially ended with the remnants of the NVA/VC force there fleeing the city, a Marine patrol, dispatched from the combat base to see how closely the NVA were entrenched, was ambushed and nearly wiped out just a few hundred meters away. Nineteen American bodies would not be recovered for over a month because of the continuing presence of hundreds of NVA troops in that area. This tragedy would later be referred to in Khe Sanh lore as "The Ghost Patrol." Word of the successful ambush, which their political officers spun as a major American "counterattack," boosted the morale of the NVA soldiers encircling Khe Sanh.[67]

* * *

Low clouds and fog closed the airfield to all but a few landings from fixed-wing aircraft. Those that tried to land, ran a gauntlet of antiaircraft fire on the way in and out. Once on the runway, mortar and artillery rounds chased them along. Several aircraft were shot down, including a U.S. Air Force C-123 killing all forty-nine people onboard, many of them Marines and Navy corpsmen returning from prior medical evacuations. Following that tragedy, the airstrip was closed, and Khe Sanh now received supplies by way of parachute drops and helicopters.

The NVA did not use bomber or attack aircraft against Khe Sanh, as was widely rumored they might, but their artillery was relentless, with the combat base receiving hundreds of rounds of incoming artillery each day—some days exceeding a thousand.

The NVA guns had a range of up to nineteen miles, while the largest Marine artillery pieces at Khe Sanh base had a range of only nine miles. So, while their shells could reach us, we could not hit them back. Therefore, they set up artillery firebases in a broad arc to the south and west, just out of range of American artillery, and always protected by antiaircraft guns.

In the months leading up to the siege, the NVA had created numerous potential artillery positions and, to avoid detection, would move their guns frequently from place to place, often pulled by motor vehicles whose tire tracks they were careful to brush away. They were also careful to keep these artillery positions away from concentrations of infantry, supply dumps, communications bunkers, etc., to avoid suffering collateral damage from attacks on those targets.

The most notorious of the NVA artillery fire on Khe Sanh base came from the Co Roc Massif in Laos, an enormous limestone cliff facing east, pocked with numerous large caves. Within these caves, the NVA installed some of their big guns which would be rolled forward to fire and then returned into the cave for safety from U.S. observation aircraft.

The northerners' forward observation posts on high ground around the combat base would assess damage and casualties from the artillery fire and radio back to their batteries the location of new targets of opportunity, such as men congregating in the open. We defenders soon tuned into the rhythm of the incoming barrages and planned our travels around the base in short dashes from one piece of cover to another, lest enemy observers spot us standing in one place too long.

Captain Baig frequently mocked the NVA for their antiquated "First World War artillery tactics." Indeed, Khe Sanh did have a First World War feel, with the fog and drizzle; muddy, rat-infested bunkers; parallel trench systems; constant reciprocal shelling of one another; and the occasional costly forays across a short, shell-pocked "No Man's Land."[68]

An NVA campaign history of the siege notes how they intended to "liberate" Khe Sanh: "The Ninth Regiment would be reinforced by sappers who would attack along the primary direction from the south and southeast and the Sixty-Sixth Regiment would attack at the west and southwest and the Twenty-Fourth Regiment would be a reserve force."[69]

Thus, four thousand NVA troops, many hundreds of them already dug in close to the base, would be in on the assault, assisted by tanks and artillery. Khe Sanh's six thousand defenders were spread thin around the combat base and outposts. The primary direction of this NVA attack would come from the south, concentrating on an area defended by just a few hundred Marines and ARVN rangers. After NVA combat engineers had cleared paths though the mine fields, and blown holes in the defensive barbed wire with Bangalore torpedoes, Ninth Regiment assault troops would rise out of their nearby bunkers, and a protective ravine just one hundred yards from the defenders, flooding through the darkness into the combat base by the thousands.

Such an assault would put these invaders at the doorstep of the regimental command bunker within minutes, so Captain Baig began concentrating on that area to keep them from massing in such numbers, later writing: "Here was felt the most weight of the Mini- and Micro-Arc Lights; here were fired the majority of the artillery clearance fires."[70] Enemy siege works in this area were more densely established than anywhere else on the battlefield, a jumble of bunker complexes, trenches and connectors. "So intensely did the NVA prepare this ground," Baig said, "that targets ceased to be regarded individually—instead *ground* was the target."

Once Colonel Lownds accepted that proposition, Baig subjected the area, at five hundred to fifteen hundred meters outside the Marine perimeter, to saturation air and artillery bombardment, saying: "The fact that the enemy never altered his intentions for this scenario [to launch a massive assault on the base] is further indication of his inflexibility and rigidity."[71]

Despite this murderous bombardment, the NVA clung to the combat base. Those who survived were replaced every two weeks by fresh troops from the rear area to avoid mental breakdown resulting from the stress. An NVA unit history later boasted that, throughout this unimaginable ordeal, their soldiers employed smokeless cookers to enjoy hot meals each day, and Division-level health officers regularly visited to spray their vermin-infested bunkers with pesticide.[72] Political officers built up their confidence by reminding them that, because of their close proximity to the Americans, they were being spared from the dreaded B-52 bombings, and, in that way, were luckier than their comrades farther from the base.

While the NVA had learned this technique for avoiding Arc Lights during fighting at Con Thien four months earlier; the Americans came away from that September experience with an equally valuable lesson learned. Ironically, this was the result of a nearly catastrophic mistake, when one of the over nine hundred B-52 bombing sorties that month sent to slow the NVA buildup around Con Thein, inadvertently struck an area *less than a mile* from the camp—without doing serious harm to the Marines there.[73]

American military planners quickly recognized the significance of that blunder, and now understood that, to save Khe Sanh, this restriction must be lifted; and the criteria loosened for allowing inbound B-52s to be diverted to other targets in tactical emergencies. On February 13, 1968, General Westmoreland advised his superior in Honolulu, Admiral Ulysses S. Grant Sharp Jr., Commander-in-Chief, Pacific Command, that the situation had become so dire there was no other alternative.

Sharp delayed granting this permission, pending a controlled measure of assurance that such a significant policy change would not injure the American and ARVN troops defending Khe Sanh. A test bombing was ordered to take place about three quarters of a mile from Hill 881 South. To mitigate possible concussion and damage to their eardrums, the Marines there were commanded to stay in their bunkers with fingers in their ears and jaws wide open throughout the bombing. As had happened at Con Thein, no severe physical problems resulted, although a few Marines suffered nosebleeds due to the sharp, instantaneous rise in ambient atmospheric pressure from the explosions.[74] The Admiral granted permission on February 18.

On February 27, two days after the Ghost Patrol was ambushed, the NVA, evidently unaware of that game-changing test, and still confident the Americans would remain inflexible concerning the three-thousand-meter restriction, massed their troops and tanks around Khe Sanh village, ready to join forces with hundreds of their comrades entrenched closer to the Marine lines, in a massive human wave attack to capture the combat base.

As the hours ticked by, the fate of the Marines grew more uncertain. Then, at that most critical moment in Khe Sanh's survival, Colonel Lownds received an encrypted message from Third Marine Division headquarters granting permission to target Arc Light strikes as close as necessary to save the base. Captain Baig had up-to-the minute target map coordinates ready.

However, one more restriction stood in his way. A month earlier, Colonel Lownds had refused to allow in several hundred Montagnard civilians seeking safety at the combat base, fearful that VC and NVA soldiers might be mingling among them. Instead, he sent them back down the road to the village with his promise that they would be protected, and ordered Captain Baig not to shoot artillery or drop bombs on their hamlets.

Baig obeyed, using a grease pencil to draw circles on his map transparency around the areas where they lived, labeling them as "no-fire zones."

But, upon receiving permission to use B-52s closer to the base, Baig erased those grease-pencil markings with a small piece of cheese cloth and ordered emergency Arc Lights which obliterated the area. While this bombing undoubtedly preempted the mass assault, it also killed an estimated one thousand civilian Montagnard living adjacent to the area where the NVA were staging for their attack.

Surprisingly to me, Colonel Lownds seemed to have been unaware that Baig had targeted the village area. Just two weeks earlier, Lownds told a *New York Times* correspondent that he had experienced some misgivings about sending so many civilians back to the village after they had come to the combat base for refuge, concluding: "This thing can come back to haunt me—all of us."[75]

Upon being advised of the Arc Light on Khe Sanh village, Lownds stormed into the FSCC room. I had never seen him so angry. "Harry," he shouted. "I understand that you bombed the ville?" Captain Baig courteously replied, "Yes, Sir." Lownds reminded him that he had forbidden it. Baig calmly explained the necessity of having to do it as the only way to spare the combat base from an enormous assault, and then stood stoically silent.

I will never forget the look on the colonel's face. It was part anger at the insubordination, and part resignation to the fact that it was done, and there was nothing he could now do about it. He stared silently at Baig for several moments and then said, quite seriously: "Harry, I wouldn't want to be you when the war crimes trials start." The colonel then turned and left the room.

After his bombing of the Montagnards, some enlisted men in the command bunker dubbed the captain "Butcher Baig." While this label spread quickly among troops across the base, I do not recall it ever being used in his presence.

On February 29, 1968, two days after the terrible Arc Light destruction at Khe Sanh village which had preempted a major attack, NVA forces readied for another attempt to take the combat base, attacking from the south and southeast. Intelligence reports described a sudden and rapid logistical buildup, with significantly increased traffic coming out of Laos toward Khe Sanh. An airborne observer reported a steady vehicle traffic heading along Route 9 toward the combat base.

Spotlight reports began to stack up on Captain Baig's desk. Colonel Lownds later recalled feeling that "this might well be the main attack," and requested immediate Arc Lights; warning Division headquarters that if they took longer than two hours to arrive, it would likely be too late because the enemy would then be engaged with his defenders.[76]

The B-52s arrived in time and Lownds later reported they destroyed "at least two battalions." Since the Marines were already in contact with an entire battalion dug in closely to the combat base, it appeared this was to have been a regimental-size attack, about fifteen hundred troops.[77] Some members of the South Vietnamese Thirty-Seventh Ranger Company, whose trench lines extended precariously outside the combat base, reported a ghastly rain of enemy body parts floating down on them.

Apparently, the NVA High Command still had not surmised from the bombing test near Hill 881 South or the February 27 Arc Light on Khe Sanh village, that the three-thousand-meter restriction was no longer being enforced. Or perhaps they did, but given the rigidity of their methods, could not (or would not) change the plan in time to save an entire regiment of crack assault forces from destruction on February 29. This would prove to be the closest Arc Light ever intentionally targeted by the Americans. Not since our ammo dump exploded in January, had the base rocked like that. In the command bunker, roof beams groaned and dust sifted down onto us.

The next day, March 1, remnants of that once-powerful NVA assault force, still adhering to their original orders, made a halfhearted attempt to overrun the Ranger position, but were easily repulsed. On March 22, the NVA would attempt one more, ultimately unsuccessful, effort to capture the base. The siege of Khe Sanh "officially" ended on April 5, but with approximately seven thousand North Vietnamese soldiers still in the general vicinity, that event was more media hype than real.

> **YOU ARE TOLD:**
> US war escalation in Vietnam, intensification of attacks on the Democratic Republic of Vietnam, shelling of the North by long-range guns positioned south of the 17th parallel — all this is aimed at protecting the lives of GIs in Vietnam.
>
> **BUT WHAT YOU ACTUALLY GET IS:**
> — More bloody fighting along Highway 9;
> — More artillery pounding of your posts, gun emplacements and bases in Gio-linh, Dong-ha, Da-nang, etc.
> — Consequently: More American casualties and more sorrow for American families.
> For every step taken by Johnson in escalating and intensifying the war either in North or South Vietnam shall meet with deserved punishment.
>
> FOR GIs IN VIETNAM
> the only way to save their lives is to:
> — Refuse to take part in mop-ups and rescue operations!
> — Demand their immediate repatriation!
> — Let themselves be captured by the Liberation forces! All prisoners will be given humane treatment.
>
> *Truyền đơn đánh cho lính Mỹ*

In addition to the thousands of English-language POW instruction pamphlets the NVA had waiting for the defenders of Khe Sanh, they would frequently provide the Americans with propaganda leaflets during the siege, urging them to surrender. These were most often delivered by incoming artillery shells fused to explode in the air over the base. (*Author's artifact*)

French Union Army trenchline at Dien Bien Phu just before the base fell in May 1954. *(National Archives and Records Administration)*

U.S. Marine trenchline at Khe Sanh in February 1968. Members of the Frist Battalion, Twenty-Sixth Marines wait for a human wave attack from the south. An NVA battalion is entrenched just beyond the road. *(Kyoichi Sawada)*

Entrance to the Dien Bien Phu command bunker just after being captured by Giap's forces in May 1954. (*People's Army of Vietnam*)

Colonel Lownds at the entrance to Khe Sanh command bunker in February 1968. Note the ongoing sandbag repair project, with the clean, new layer on the right side, contrasted with the older sandbags on the left — all heavily damaged from NVA incoming artillery and mortar shells. (*Author's photograph*)

Khe Sanh Combat Base. The one-hundred-and-fifty-meter-long road from the base down to the water collection reservoir (located at about 5 o'clock in photo) is clearly visible. The North Vietnamese Army, who controlled this area throughout the siege, apparently failed to understand the significance of this reservoir, and the small pipe running back to the base. This was the only source of water for the defenders, a major vulnerability for the Americans that could have swung the battle. *(National Archives and Records Administration)*

11
HARD LUCK

The question remains: Exactly what were Hanoi's intentions when they surrounded the Khe Sanh Combat Base and its outposts in early-1968 with nearly thirty-thousand troops?

Even before the siege ended, some suggested it had all been a clever deception from the beginning. Never intending to capture the base, the NVA used these elaborate resource-intensive maneuverings as a decoy to strengthen their hand elsewhere during the Tet Offensive by tying up thousands of American and South Vietnamese troops and valuable aviation resources.

In the decades since this "decoy" theory took hold, enough declassified U.S. military and North Vietnamese records have come to light, including memoirs by influential NVA military leaders, to make a compelling argument that capturing the Khe Sanh Combat Base, in a duplication of their famous victory over the French at Dien Bien Phu fourteen years earlier, was not an incidental aspiration by the NVA, but a fixation—one they continued pursuing long after the Tet Offensive had failed throughout the rest of the country, making an ongoing deception unnecessary.

Primary among the reasons that bound them to the goal of seizing Khe Sanh, and with it potentially many hundreds of American captives, was the enormous propaganda value of such a humiliating defeat for the Americans. This, in what was shaping up to be a contentious U.S. election year, would create enormous public pressure for a quick negotiated settlement, just as the fall of Dien Bien Phu had done in reshaping the government in France.

But, there was another, more practical, reason for wanting the base gone. As the CIA had noted in January 1968, "the communists have long regarded Khe Sanh, located near the infiltration corridor into Laos, as a thorn in their side."⁷⁸ It was precisely the same reason they had tried to take the base in May 1967. The proximity of Khe Sanh required the NVA to permanently tie up thousands of security forces along the Ho Chi Minh Trail; forces that would otherwise be on the offensive elsewhere. The NVA also feared, and Westmoreland repeatedly fanned those fears, that Khe Sanh was a perfect staging point for an invasion of their supply depots deeper inside Laos (which eventually occurred in January–March 1971). So, the question might be asked: Who was tying up who?

Those of us who were there during the siege had no doubt about our enemy's intentions. Officers in the Khe Sanh command center, who possessed the most complete information from intelligence reports on what the NVA were doing outside the base, knew just how ominous the situation was. Captain Steen later noted, "We were all very concerned. I don't think people realize just how close it was."⁷⁹ Baig concurred, noting that the NVA possessed the modern weaponry and the well-equipped and disciplined infantry to have repeated Dien Bien Phu, but a rigid adherence to antiquated methodology became its Achilles heel.⁸⁰ "Had the NVA been capable of our artillery techniques," Baig said, "they could and would have blown us out of Khe Sanh."⁸¹

Early on, Baig recognized the enemy's unrelenting pursuit of a tactical reenactment of Dien Bien Phu on the Khe Sanh battlefield. This was evident in the timing of their early incremental assaults on the outposts and their subsequent and predictable method of constructing trenches, bunker complexes, parallels, and saps around the base.

Despite continuous artillery fire, close-in air support with napalm and high explosives, and countless Arc Light strikes, the encircling enemy troops persisted in rebuilding and advancing their traditional networks on the approaches to the combat base. Baig later commented:

> The ant-like mentality of the enemy apparently made them continue rebuilding. What we were concerned with primarily was an enemy rush on the wire. We never thought the enemy would fight in quite the inept way he did. We really thought we could expect mass, human-wave attacks.⁸²

Hanoi's fixation with Khe Sanh seems especially obvious after it became clear in the first week of February that the dream of a popular civilian uprising in support of their forces would not materialize as it had at Dien Bien Phu when hundreds of thousands of peasants volunteered food, services and labor in that effort. Le Duan badly misjudged support for his forces in the south, stranding many hundreds of troops in places like Hué and Saigon, without a chance of holding the ground they had initially captured; sending thousands more—now demoralized that most of the civilian population had rejected them—racing in a panic from pursuing forces back to sanctuaries in Cambodia and Laos.

The absence of that uprising made the capture of Khe Sanh even more important to Le Duan and his clique, as evidenced by the obscene cost, in terms of casualties, weapons and materiel so precious to Hanoi's ongoing war effort, they were willing to expend while repeatedly staging for large scale attacks on the base throughout February and March.

Earlier, in the fall of 1967, while Hanoi prepared to move forward with its enormous investment at Khe Sanh of nearly an entire army corps (over twenty-seven thousand infantry and support troops), a single Marine infantry battalion defended the combat base and its aviation and artillery support contingents. It would be ludicrous to argue that such an overwhelming force was necessary to pin down less than two thousand Marines. As the NVA plan of attack unfolded, Westmoreland rushed another four thousand troops to defend Khe Sanh. Even if Hanoi had anticipated such a move, it does not explain their willingness to continue feeding so many reinforcements on to the battlefield to mask a ruse. A CIA analysis concluded that between late-January and early-April 1968, NVA losses ranged from 50 to 65 percent of the personnel committed to the Khe Sanh operation, including replacements, which averaged from one hundred ninety to three hundred eighty troops per day. Thus, the total number of NVA troops engaged in battle over that seventy-seven-day period may have exceeded forty-four thousand—an extraordinary commitment merely to disguise a deception.[83]

By early February, American and ARVN forces at Khe Sanh were outnumbered, cut off from the rest of the country by land, and hindered from airborne resupply due to dense ground fog and antiaircraft fire. The tactical progression of the NVA advance, which brought their trenchlines within a few hundred meters of the combat base, was a clear emulation of Dien Bien Phu. So, why were they unable to finish the job?

The answer lies in examining an absurd series of mishaps, flukes of incredibly bad luck, and appalling security blunders—all beginning in the dark, early hours of January 2, 1968. On that morning, a Marine guard in a hidden listening post just outside the western perimeter of the combat base, observed a group of six people apparently surveying potential avenues of attack. Other Marines were dispatched to the scene and when the intruders, now standing stiffly in the darkness, did not respond to a verbal challenge, the Americans opened fire and then retreated to their lines. At first light they returned to find five dead NVA soldiers (a bloody trail away from the site indicated one may have escaped alive). Later examination of their clothing, equipment and weapons led Marine intelligence officers to conclude that at least three were high ranking officers, a regimental commander, operations officer and communications officer. An analysis later stated: "That the North Vietnamese would commit such key men to an extremely dangerous personal reconnaissance indicated that Khe Sanh was a priority."[84]

More bad luck befell them just twelve days later, when a Marine reconnaissance patrol, in the same area where the Hill Fights had taken place eight months earlier, surprised and skirmished with a large NVA unit whose guards had not been alert to their approach. This NVA infantry unit was in the process of positioning itself for the scheduled attack on Khe Sanh base in three weeks and believed, incorrectly, it was well-enough hidden to avoid detection.

Preparations by the NVA for capturing Khe Sanh were to have been completed in the first week of February, the plan calling for an all-out rush on the outposts and then the combat base. But news of this encounter with the Marine patrol panicked the High Command into moving the date of attack up three weeks to January 20—now just five days away—setting off frantic movements of soldiers, ammunition and food to forward staging areas.

The NVA 304th Division History states:

> On January 20, 1968, the rear services bases had just been established and that was [now] the date of the opening fire for the campaign. Because time to prepare was short and the units had arrived late, the preparations for campaigns supply stock as well as the tactics to be employed encountered difficulty. The system of campaign depots, transportation effort, the assets of the campaign military medical system, could not begin on time.[85]

Yet, the decision by the NVA High Command to impulsively change the timetable, ultimately depriving the initial assault forces of vital support services and supplies, may have been as much a product of overconfidence as it was anxiety. The Vietnamese victory at Dien Bien Phu had been due in part to the smugness and complacency of French generals who considered their adversary inferior and thus incapable of defeating a western industrialized nation with a peasant army.

But now it seemed it was the NVA who were brimming with self-assurance, perhaps arrogance, that they would make quick work of Khe Sanh, and a defending American force they considered to be inferior fighters due to an over-reliance on air power; an advantage they would neutralize by swiftly moving into close quarters with their enemy. There is no better illustration of this disdain for the fighting ability of their American foes than in the bundles of English language pamphlets they brought with them to the front, containing surrender instructions for the thousands of POWs they would soon be processing. Baig and his fellow FSCC officers recognized signs of this overconfidence early on. "The NVA made some big mistakes." Captain Steen later wrote. "They underestimated us." [86]

Such condescension is understandable given the sheer size of the attack force and caliber of troops sent against Khe Sanh. While most communist military forces fighting in Hué, and other cities during Tet, were local VC units, only at Khe Sanh did they commit divisions of their most highly trained and best equipped troops. In addition to regiments of infantry, only at Khe Sanh did they bring forward so many specialized support troops, including artillery, anti-aircraft and tank regiments; and battalions of porters, medical technicians, radio and telephone communications experts, supply personal, vehicle maintenance and fuel specialists, combat and construction engineers, and high-level command-and-control administrative staffs.

Such a large, complex force would have been more in keeping with a mission to inflict permanent military defeat and remain to occupy that part of the country. While there is no way to determine at this time, whether the Khe Sanh invasion force included a specific political component to govern western Quang Tri province once the base fell, we do know that this was an element of Hanoi's master plan for the Offensive. Not surprisingly, a U.S. Army unit during the battle for control of Hué city, captured a group of Vietnamese attempting to enter the city—who turned out to be the new provisional communist government.[87]

Whatever the case, those who descended on the isolated and outnumbered forces at Khe Sanh in January 1968 believed they were participating in a significant moment in their nation's military history—one not seen since the glorious victory at Dien Bien Phu.

***

But Khe Sanh appears not to have been Hanoi's first choice. Just two months earlier, they sent four regiments, about 6,000 troops, against the American Army base and airfield at Dak To, about two hundred miles to the south, in the mountains along South Vietnam's border with Laos and Cambodia. Like at Khe Sanh, the NVA had been preparing the area around Dak To for over a year with heavily fortified bunkers, trench complexes and enormous quantities of supplies and ammunition. Also like at Khe Sanh, fighting in the hills around the base was intense, with some of the bloodiest of the war taking place on Hill 875.

In early November, when the NVA moved in to capture the base, the similarities with Khe Sanh were even more striking. North Vietnamese rockets in the initial moments of the attack struck an ammo dump exploding eleven hundred tons of ordnance, and destroyed cargo planes and helicopters on the ground. As with Khe Sanh, a timely defector had provided important information about the North Vietnamese order of battle, helping the Americans repel the assault. It was not until over four thousand additional U.S. troops arrived to assist the one thousand defenders, that the NVA finally went on the defensive and eventually retired into their sanctuaries across the border. A captured NVA document told of Hanoi's strategy; one that was not simply a diversion, but rather "to annihilate a major U.S. element" in order to force the Americans and ARVN to deploy additional forces to remote areas of the country away from the population centers.

While this strategy did encourage General Westmoreland to move more troops to the hinterlands, several members of his staff thought they saw similarities between this attack and Dien Bien Phu, and evidence the NVA had gone to Dak To prepared to stay.

American intelligence reports later confirmed that the NVA units who fought there were so badly mauled that they were unable to participate in the upcoming Tet Offensive. This information fanned the discussion of why the NVA had expended so many of their forces, if not to capture Dak To. However, such theorizing about similarities to Dien Bien Phu was given little credence until several weeks later when Khe Sanh came under siege, this time not by one NVA division, as in their failed effort at Dak To, but nearly three divisions, including thousands of support troops. Suddenly the words of the captured NVA document "to annihilate a major U.S. element" had everyone's attention.

A successful model of the attack plan Hanoi devised for Khe Sanh was finally achieved just a few weeks after the siege there ended. In May, two NVA regiments moved on Kham Duc, an isolated American camp and airfield about half way between Dak To and Khe Sanh, deep in the mountains near the Laotian border. Intelligence information about the NVA buildup had prompted General Westmoreland to begin upgrading the airstrip and fortifying the defenses, as he had at Khe Sanh late the previous year. Once again, the general was convinced he could destroy a numerically superior enemy with an intense artillery and bombing campaign. However, when over two thousand NVA soldiers—unimpeded by the calamities and frequent ineptitude their forces experienced at Khe Sanh—swiftly overran surrounding outposts and took the high ground above the Kham Duc airfield, Westmoreland reluctantly ordered the evacuation of all three-thousand military and civilian inhabitants.

Two days after abandoning it, sixty B-52 bombers obliterated the camp. It was the worst U.S. military defeat of the war, a product of Westmoreland's insistence on defending such remote "prestige" positions. Except for the NVA's disastrous luck at Khe Sanh, Kham Duc might have been the second of two inconceivable and humiliating American military reverses on the battlefield in Vietnam—just a few weeks apart.

At Khe Sanh, the implausible string of hard luck would continue to dog the NVA after hastily moving up the date of the attack on Khe Sanh to January 21. Just hours before the first assaults were to be launched, Lieutenant La Thanh Tonc surrendered at the east end of the Khe Sanh airfield under a white flag. Tonc, who commanded an anti-aircraft artillery battery, and was disgruntled due to lack of promotion, gave up an incredible amount of intelligence information not only about the upcoming attack on Khe Sanh, but the forthcoming nationwide offensive that would begin in ten days. It was initially believed Tonc was a "plant" sent over intentionally to misdirect the defenders' plans, but Captain Baig thought otherwise:

> The enemy never deviated from the plan that Ton [sic] provided us. Ton's revelations of the concept of operations, prior and detailed knowledge of NVA and methodology, the requirements of siege warfare, and the lessons of Dien Bien Phu and Con Thien, gave us all the information we needed to plan the nature of our supporting arms and countermeasures.[88]

Tonc also revealed a related plan involving attacks on the Dong Ha and Quang Tri airfields, forty miles to the east, on the morning of January 21 to prevent helicopters there from assisting at Khe Sanh. Before arriving at the combat base, Baig, and his counterintelligence teams out of Dong Ha, established a collection of spy networks far into North Vietnam "that had penetrated several NVA headquarters and other organizations."[89] As such, Baig was able to quickly identify the rocket artillery regiment tasked with destroying the helicopters on the ground, and had them annihilated by artillery and naval gunfire as they moved into position.

On January 20, just after Tonc surrendered, another incredible stroke of misfortune befell the NVA when a patrol from the Marine outpost on Hill 881 South, five miles west of the combat base, by sheer chance ran into several hundred enemy troops moving into position to attack the hill after night fall. Before becoming encircled and trapped, the Marines fought their way back up to the safety of their defensive positions and prepared to repel the coming assault.

Having lost the element of surprise, the NVA decided not to attack Hill 881 South. Instead, they sent about five hundred soldiers to capture a different outpost nearby, Hill 861. What the NVA commanders evidently did not consider when they changed plans, was that this decision freed up the Marines on 881 South to unleash the artillery and mortar fire that they would otherwise have used in their own defense, directly on those now trying to capture Hill 861. Hill 881 South would fire over a thousand rounds, annihilating the NVA reserves waiting to finish off the Marine defenders on 861—likely saving that critical outpost from falling.

If the Marines on Hill 881 South had not accidently crossed paths that day with the large enemy force advancing on them, the NVA may have recaptured both these hills that they had lost in battle the previous spring, and once again held the western high ground overlooking the airstrip and combat base. Such an unnerving replication of their timetable in rolling up the hill outposts around Dien Bien Phu, would have put Khe Sanh base in that same grave jeopardy.

In the first light of day on January 21, just as the devastated NVA battalion was falling back from their thwarted attack on Hill 861, about seven hundred of their comrades assaulted the South Vietnamese government's district headquarters in Khe Sanh village two miles from the combat base, guarded by a relatively weak contingent of American and indigenous forces.

After two days of fighting, and just before running out of ammunition, the defenders abandoned the headquarters compound and made their way to the combat base. Hanoi would proudly proclaim its first capture of a South Vietnamese seat of government in the war. But NVA military records later reported it had cost them six hundred forty casualties, of whom one hundred fifty-four were killed[90] (the defenders' causalities were negligible by comparison). Given such an enormous loss of life in an effort in which the NVA should have easily overrun so few defenders, the acclaimed capture of the district headquarters was literally a Pyrrhic victory.

The reason for so many NVA casualties in that fight was yet another example of bungling and misfortune. While on their five-mile march on January 20 to get into position to capture the district headquarters compound around midnight, the battalion became separated and many lost their way. Most of the troops eventually arrived at their destination late and exhausted, just as the sun was rising. Though still in disarray, they quickly attacked and were decimated by prearranged artillery airbursts above the defensive perimeter—a standard American defensive artillery practice that they appear not to have anticipated. Their battalion commander was killed in the barrage and his entire staff was so badly wounded that a company-level political officer, himself bleeding, and with a broken arm, directed the remainder of the attack. To make matters worse, due to the accelerated schedule for launching the assault, decided upon just five days before, they had only half the ammunition and rations they needed.[91]

12
THE BUNGLED DIEN BIEN PHU

Probably the greatest misunderstanding about the siege — one that gave rise to the idea that the NVA did not intend to capture the combat base — is the mistaken belief that they never launched a major ground assault against it. Historical records clearly contradict that notion. In fact, it was the Americans' effectiveness in breaking up repeated attempts to capture the main base, that resulted in the idea that those attacks were neither planned nor executed.

Throughout February and March, as described in earlier chapters, Baig and his fellow fire support officers in the command center engaged in the systematic, daily destruction of NVA equipment, fortifications and infantry units. Often, like the fifteen hundred-person strong Ninth Regiment on February 6; or the tank-reinforced infantry battalion assembling in nearby Khe Sanh village on February 27; or another fifteen-hundred-person, human wave assault on the southeast perimeter on February 29, they were blown to bits by Arc Lights as they moved in to capture Khe Sanh base.

Few knew at the time that there had been another significant NVA defector besides Lieutenant Tonc. On January 22, two days after Tonc's surrender, Private Lai Van Minh approached the base from the northeast with his hands in the air. Minh said he was defecting from a transportation company supporting a nearby infantry regiment, and furnished information about his unit and the nature of recent truck shipments. He also informed his interrogators that a political officer recently told those in his company that if the initial January attacks on Khe Sanh failed, the NVA would pull many of their units back into Laos to regroup.

Then, on February 3, three days into the nationwide Tet Offensive, and with all the originally scheduled units and support elements finally in place around Khe Sanh, they would renew their efforts to capture the outposts and the combat base, this time with twice the number of troops used in the premature attacks on January 21, along with artillery support and tanks.

In addition, Minh's company commander told them that "Khe Sanh would be for the Americans what Dien Bien Phu had been for the French," and that, after taking the combat base, NVA troops would press on to the east until all American and ARVN fortifications along Route 9 were captured.[92] The commander further told them not to worry about B-52 attacks, because they would move so close to the Marines, that the U.S. Air Force would be unwilling to risk using those kinds of airstrikes.

Minh's American interrogators, at first, were skeptical of how a lowly private could know so much, and thought him to be a disinformation "plant." However, less than two weeks later—on the night of February 3— the NVA moved about one thousand troops into position to attack Hill 881 South and Hill 861 Alpha—just as Minh described hearing from his superiors in early January.

Part of that NVA plan was successful the following day, when they used tanks to capture the U.S. Army Special Forces Camp at Lang Vei. However, they again failed to capture the hill outposts because this time the Marines were prepared; and, their February 6 regimental-size attack on the Khe Sanh Combat Base was decimated because Baig was waiting with Arc Lights.

***

Despite the NVA's episodes of bad luck, ineptitude, spies, and the untimely and ruinous intelligence information provided by defectors, they still might have been successful had it not been for their egregious violations of basic radio security. The Vietnamese-speaking operators in the U.S. Army's FOB-3 compound, and more distant signal intelligence units, monitored radio transmissions from nearby enemy units throughout the siege and continuously shared that information with the Marines in the command bunker. These intercepts frequently appalled Captain Baig's sense of professionalism:

> The enemy's radio discipline was bad and he talked openly about many things from the mundane to the highly classified. On one occasion, a commander, or at least his radio operator, asked another radio operator: 'Where is the mobile brothel? It hasn't arrived. Another fellow was running a black market over the radio, setting up times and meeting places for the exchanges.[93]

The "highly classified" radio conversations included unencrypted discussions of major tactical plans, including locations and time tables. These radio intercepts, coupled with information from Montagnard spies, and the probability of well-placed informants within the upper ranks of the NVA, previously groomed by Baig and his divisional counterintelligence operatives, led to the early elimination of many high-level officers and their staffs, crippling their chains-of-command at a time when precision and consistency were most required, keeping NVA forces around Khe Sanh weakened and confused.

Just four days after Baig's arrival, an intercepted radio message identified an NVA artillery headquarters south of the base. The coordinates, he later wrote, were in Vietnamese and once translated "offered three or four different formulas, each one giving us three or four different answers. So, we took the one that their *highest* headquarters indicated to be correct." He was able to divert an Arc Light over the site within three hours and "blew up a fantastic amount of the countryside." The air strike resulted in over thirty secondary explosions.

Another such strike occurred just a week later when Baig and his team learned the time of a Division-level meeting of staffs and commanders taking place at a schoolhouse in a village near the border with Laos. Twenty minutes after the meeting was scheduled to start, fighter-bombers dropped one hundred fifty bombs in concert with artillery batteries from Khe Sanh base, and distant Camp Carroll and the Rockpile, firing a total of three hundred fifty rounds. Baig would drolly recall that he put together this deadly tandem of fire "to welcome the delegates, targeting a five hundred meter by three-hundred-meter square around the schoolhouse to take in the hangers-on and other idlers who usually congregate around large staffs."[94] Later, this "performance" would be repeated against another staff meeting being held about five miles south of that now-obliterated school house.

An NVA military history provides a graphic account of another of Baig's strikes on an artillery battalion headquarters complex several miles from the base:

> During the most savage phase of the siege, when enemy jets and B-52s were being used in place of artillery support, the rear was not any safer than the front lines. During one B-52 strike bombs hit the area where the battalion headquarters was located and a number of bunkers collapsed. After the bomb explosions ended, everyone feverishly began to dig to rescue the wounded, they found five dead bodies. Every one of those killed was very young, between 18 and 20 years old. They were all new high school graduates who had volunteered to join the fight. [95]

One of those killed was the battalion commander's personal assistant: "This young man had been exempt from the draft, but he had volunteered and had done everything he could to join the army. When his body was dug out from the earth no one who saw him could keep from crying."

The most significant of these attacks on NVA high-level staff occurred after a Marine signal intelligence unit identified an unusually high volume of radio traffic emanating from the tiny village of Sat Lit in Laos. The massive January 30 bombing of that campaign headquarters, described in an earlier chapter, permanently silenced all radio transmissions from the site.

For much of that following week, concerned that the Americans had violated the security of their entire radio network, the NVA resorted to the most primitive form of military communication: runners. Carrying messages to dozens of large and small-unit headquarters, these runners pushed through rugged mountain and jungle terrain for fifteen to twenty miles, then returned with replies.[96] This breakdown in communication across the campaign front, coming at a time when the NVA were anticipating great success rolling up additional American outposts around Khe Sanh, dramatically slowed their momentum.

The NVA High Command agonized over the security failure, describing the organization of the campaign command as "simplistic, wrong, and subjective. Secrecy was lost... headquarters equipment was rudimentary and compromised."[97]

* * *

Some historians have offered as evidence that the NVA never intended to capture Khe Sanh Combat Base the facts they did not cut the telephone landline to the outside; nor interrupt the defender's sole source of water, which was pumped through a two-inch pipe from a small, stream-fed reservoir, one hundred fifty meters outside the base's north defensive perimeter, in an area controlled by the besiegers.

The telephone landline presented no vulnerability for the defenders, as they had fifty-three separate radio networks assisted by six radio relay sites at various distances from the combat base that provided twenty-four-hour-a-day radio and secure teletype contact with the outside, as well as a secure microwave telephone connection and encrypted radio voice circuit to division headquarters, and beyond.[98]

The issue of water was more significant. Some have speculated the North Vietnamese did not know where the water pipe was located, but this is highly unlikely since they, or civilian spies, must have observed the small reservoir from which water was drawn being created the previous October by heavy construction equipment driven from the combat base.[99]

Perhaps the NVA did not recognize this pipe as being the *sole* source of water for the Marines, who had tried unsuccessfully to dig water wells within the base in November 1967,[100] just as the NVA were gearing up to attack. It is unlikely NVA observation posts, less than two miles away on a high mountain to the north, missed seeing the drilling machinery at work. Despite the wells coming up dry, it is possible the NVA assumed they had not.

Yet, even this theory seems to be disputed by an NVA division commander at Khe Sanh who later wrote: "The greatest problem the enemy faced was that the base did not have a water source." And, a subsequent comment would indicate he did not know about the pipe: "Every day they had to wait for nightfall to sneak out to the small stream at the end of the airfield in order to collect water. That provided the opportunity for our snipers equipped with infra-red night vision scopes to fire the bullets that ended their lives."[101]

The NVA did not seem to understand the grave consequences it would have presented the Americans had they cut off that water supply. The difficulty of packaging, transporting and delivering such enormous amounts of water to meet the needs of thousands of troops at the combat base and outposts would have been staggering. Such a scenario would have been ideal for those orchestrating the Tet Offensive from Hanoi, i.e., Marines suffering from thirst at remote Khe Sanh, requiring the diversion of valuable aerial resources away from intense fighting elsewhere in the country. Perhaps it would even trigger the opportunity for them to ambush American forces outside the base during an overland emergency effort to break the siege.

Planning for such a relief effort had begun in January 1968 as a response to President Johnson's anxiety about losing Khe Sanh. The result was a resource-intensive, 30,000-person plan, labeled Operation Pegasus, under the operational control of the U.S. Army's First Air Cavalry Division. This scheme was eventually implemented in early April 1968; but, had the NVA stopped the flow of water to the base beginning in January, Pegasus may have been needed much earlier. Contemplating such a massive relief effort during the Tet Offensive would have positioned American political and military leaders with an agonizing decision to make. It is incredible that the NVA overlooked this game-changing vulnerability.

Another missed opportunity was that, despite possessing sophisticated artillery, the NVA failed to knock out the Khe Sanh regimental command center. When it was built, American forces there could not have imagined anything larger than a small mortar being fired at the combat base, and so the depth of the bunker roof consisted of only about four feet of concrete supplemented by another two to three feet of sandbags. By comparison, the roofs of NVA command bunkers at the regimental and battalion level around Khe Sanh typically consisted of alternating layers of dirt and logs eight to nine feet deep.

The NVA knew the exact location of the command bunker as early as their initial mortar attack against Khe Sanh on January 3, 1966, and had tried to knock it out hundreds of times over the next two years with an array of guns, large mortars and rockets.

In his strategy against the NVA, Captain Baig understood how crucial it was, early on, to use concentrated artillery fire and bombs to eliminate high-level officers and their staffs, crippling their chains-of-command and leaving their forces disorganized and ineffective.

North Vietnamese artillery tacticians seemed to have understood this concept, scoring a direct hit the Twenty-Sixth Marines' First Battalion command bunker, less than two hundred meters from the regimental bunker, causing much injury and loss of life. Incredibly, they similarly destroyed that same battalion's replacement command bunker, soon after it was occupied. Also, in the first moments of the battle, on the morning of January 21, their gunners pinpointed and destroyed a hut adjacent to the regimental command bunker that Colonel Lownds used as his aboveground quarters, surely hoping to catch him at home. Moments later, they inflicted their most significant damage on the command bunker when a 122mm Katyusha rocket blew off a corner of the roof and cracked some interior walls.

Had they moved their sights just forty feet north, with a large, delay-fused artillery shell, they would have, undoubtedly, killed or wounded most of the regimental officers and interrupted the coordinated defense of the combat base and outposts for quite some time. It is impossible to understand why the NVA did not better exploit this opportunity.

Most baffling of all, was, from the beginning of the siege, a new regimental command center was being constructed a few hundred meters away, touted as being much more artillery-resistant than the current one.

The day before the regimental staff was to move in, a large artillery shell punched through the roof of that still-vacant command bunker and destroyed it.

Their failure to capitalize on such obvious and significant American vulnerabilities at Khe Sanh remains a riddle. However, later documents indicate their High Command was cognizant of such lapses in initiative. Alongside the thousands who received commendations and promotions for their actions in the Khe Sanh campaign, over four hundred, including one hundred sixty-eight Party members and eighty-five cadre, were disciplined for incidents at the platoon-level and above. This resulted in such actions as "discharge from the Party, reduction in position, reduction in rank, particularly in a number of cases where they were referred to military tribunals." Infractions warranting such punishment were often cases where officers did not take full tactical advantage of "opportune moments" that presented themselves on the battlefield. [102]

Finally, if Khe Sanh was merely an elaborate subterfuge by the NVA, as some still contend, why, once the Tet Offensive had failed, did they continue such costly, large-unit attacks on the combat base, making the need for such a deception moot? It is possible that the failure of the nationwide offensive, elsewhere in the country, encouraged Le Duan and his clique in Hanoi to step up their efforts to capture Khe Sanh, now, seemingly the only option remaining to them to wrest a major victory from their overly ambitious failed strategy in the south.

Historian Lien-Hang Nguyen believes that until the Party opens their archives, a definitive answer may not be possible. "They've released so much on the decision-making in 1967," Lien-Hang states, "but the minute you get to the failures of 1968, they haven't revealed much."[103]

* * *

While the NVA did manage to capture several of their initial objectives early on; the district headquarters in Khe Sanh village, Ban Houie Sane and Lang Vei; they failed to take critical hills west of the base. Despite missing these key elements in the progression of their plan, Baig knew they would refuse to acknowledge such significant setbacks and rigidly adhere to the original scheme to capture the combat base.

No sadder example is found of this obvious disconnect between the reality of the Khe Sanh battlefield and Hanoi's ruinous obsession with capturing the combat base, than what appears in their own records. On March 11, campaign headquarters directed the Third Battalion, Ninth Regiment to replace their First Battalion in front of Khe Sanh's east and southeast perimeter, with orders to "seize and control the entire Marine trench line east of the airfield within one month."[104] The plan was "to dig underground trenches the same way we did when we attacked French troops defending Hill Eliane 2 [an outpost at Dien Bien Phu] with many teams taking turns to dig constantly, night and day."

Tragically for those NVA soldiers, Captain Baig knew what they were up to, how they were going to do it, and played them expertly. Predictably, the NVA pressed on, and General Nguyen Duc Huy later reported in his memoir that:

> Every night dozens of men were killed or wounded. However, these losses were justified by good results. Our siege trenches reached the enemy's forward trench-line ahead of schedule. There were only a few locations where a few rolls of concertina wire still blocked us. When the order to attack was given, we would use explosive charges to blast away the concertina wire. [105]

Headquarters gave the command on March 22, just a week before the siege of Khe Sanh was officially lifted, "to launch the assault to overrun and finish off the enemy force;" a force, they had been told incorrectly, that was starving and without water: "Their [the Americans'] lives hung by a thread and their situation hopeless," the commander later said. "The new Dien Bien Phu could be calculated in a matter of hours."

Although the NVA ranks were now depleted by weeks of shelling and bombing as they inched their lines closer to the base, they attacked nonetheless, running into a deadly wall of mortar and direct-fire weapons from the Khe Sanh trench lines. All their sappers were killed before completely breaching the defensive concertina wire. A later description indicates how reluctant the High Command was to call off the attack, doing so only after losing virtually the entire battalion:

> In light of the heavy casualties we had already suffered, and the fact that our prospects for being able to take the enemy's front trench-line were now rather low, the Division and the Front Headquarters ordered that our assault forces be withdrawn to our fortified bunker positions to regroup.[106]

A radio transmission intercepted by the Americans indicated that at least one NVA officer was unwilling to further sacrifice his men to this hopelessly inflexible—and by now delusional—strategy of capturing Khe Sanh. Captain Baig would later report that:

> A junior commander refused to launch the ground attack against the combat base and declined obeying a follow-up order [from Division Headquarters]. The higher up ordered the officer executed, after which the attack was launched but only in a very halfhearted manner.[107]

For these NVA soldiers, the continuing fervor by their superiors to replicate a "new Dien Bien Phu" was all too real.

13
IMPERCEPTION

The NVA High Command had always been cognizant that relief forces eventually would be sent to Khe Sanh, and that this would present them an excellent opportunity to isolate and ambush American units outside the base. When those reinforcements did arrive in early April, and Marine units at Khe Sanh base and its outposts pushed out to fight the enemy, the NVA did realize some notable successes in this plan, such as on Hill 689, two miles southwest of the base, where a Marine company was so badly mauled in an ambush they were forced to leave thirty bodies on the battlefield for nearly a week. In mid-May, the NVA overran a nearby U.S. Army artillery fire base and were back at the gates of the combat base, ready to attack a now-much-reduced number of defenders guarding the place.

After months more of bloody combat around Khe Sanh, the Americans finally decided to abandon it. The official reason given was a change to a mobile, helicopter-borne, assault strategy for defending that remote corner of South Vietnam, to be launched from more secure bases in the east.

However, the actual reason had to do with General Westmoreland's promotion to Army Chief of Staff. Westmoreland still did not want to abandon Khe Sanh, but his successor, General Creighton Abrams, did. Abrams had long believed that such an enormous investment in American troops and resources should not have been expended in defending a fixed, position with so little intrinsic value and one so geographically and tactically favorable to the enemy. On June 19, he initiated evacuation and destruction of the Khe Sanh base and all, but one, of its outposts. The task was completed on July 12, 1968, but only after weeks of terrible fighting in the surrounding hills, as the NVA sought to bloody the Americans at Khe Sanh one last time.

Despite Khe Sanh having dominated front-page world news just three months before, western media now barely mentioned the abandonment of the place, with brief announcements buried in most U.S. newspapers.

Newsweek magazine, which had featured Khe Sanh as a cover story just ten weeks before, now gave its abandonment just a half-page blurb.

Hanoi, on the other hand, devoted 70 percent of its radio broadcast time in several Asian languages over the ensuing five days to descriptions of the "American defeat" at Khe Sanh. Newspapers in Vietnamese, French and English language editions dedicated days of banner headlines and pages of detailed accounts about the final fighting. A variety of editorial cartoons were produced to gloat. One showed a caricature of a braying Marine, "USMC" printed on his uniform, with his buttocks on fire. Another depicted a stunned Lyndon Johnson fainting backwards into the arms of a waiting physician upon hearing the news.[108]

One overwrought front-page piece in the *Vietnam Weekly*, while implying their own losses had been negligible, claimed that during the battle for Ta Con (Khe Sanh), "liberation forces" killed fourteen thousand Americans, took hundreds more captive and shot down nearly five hundred aircraft. Such hyperbole by the government-controlled media helped Party leaders in Hanoi not only further obscure the failure of the Tet Offensive, but convince their people that they had made good on the promise to replicate the overwhelming 1954 victory of Dien Bien Phu at Khe Sanh.

However, viewing the battle of Khe Sanh as a fifteen-month-long engagement from the Hill Fights in April-May 1967 through the abandonment of Hill 689 in July 1968 (with a lull in the fighting between August 1967 and January 1968 to accommodate NVA regrouping and the rainy season), two thousand thirty Americans had been killed and an estimated eight thousand wounded. North Vietnamese Army losses were staggering. Estimates fluctuate wildly, but it is reasonable to believe that during this same period, NVA dead, wounded and missing exceeded fifty thousand. [109]

* * *

During the siege months, Khe Sanh base swarmed with reporters, largely because it was a relatively easy place to find an interesting war story. This was especially true for television camera crews, as the war came to them each day providing exciting footage of frightened Marines diving for cover from the ground jarring explosions of enemy artillery. Soon the portrayal of Khe Sanh as a modern-day Alamo, with defiant American boys about to be overwhelmed in a massive human wave attack, was garnering big TV ratings from rapt viewers. In February, CBS dedicated over 50 percent of its evening news coverage about the war to Khe Sanh, despite critical battles being fought at Hué, Saigon and other places throughout the country. When the apocalypse that these journalists promised did not materialize, they quickly abandoned Khe Sanh, leaving many of us defenders with the vague impression that they were slightly disappointed that we had been successful and survived.

Almost immediately, pundits began speculating it had been an elaborate deception on the part of Hanoi; that the legendary "Red Napoleon," General Giap, had once again outfoxed his adversary. Filtered through the prism of disenchantment and mistrust of the U.S. military command in Vietnam—much of it deserved—they refused to accept having just witnessed the largest and costliest battle of the war.

General Giap would later disparage Westmoreland's aptitude as a military leader. Comparing Westmoreland to his replacement, Giap said, "General Abrams...based his leadership on research; he studied his own and others' experiences to see what he could apply to the real situation here."[110] Ironically, in spite of General Westmoreland's supercilious leadership style, dubious candor, questionable decision-making ability and Giap's perceptive claim that he did not grasp "the real situation" in Vietnam, the evidence supports a conclusion that General Westmoreland had guessed correctly about Hanoi's fixation with Khe Sanh and counterpunched expertly, though some of that achievement must be attributed to the NVA's bad luck, outmoded artillery and siege practices, and inept leadership on the battlefield.

Captain Baig left Khe Sanh in April 1968, enormously frustrated at how the siege had been portrayed in the western press. For obvious security reasons, the news people were never apprised of his uncanny grasp of the

NVA's tactical temperament, nor his extraordinary comprehension of their methods. This was particularly true in his cracking the NVA blueprint for "doctrinal position area engineering," a rigid formula for laying out their emplacements.

Within the confines of the combat base, the press was unable to observe the incessant, methodical destruction raining down upon the NVA, systematically destroying vital supply and other support facilities and decimating battalion after battalion as they repeatedly staged for the conclusive attack. Exasperated, Baig later wrote:

> The artillery initiative was ours, and we held it throughout the siege, despite the worst croaking of sundry, inexperienced correspondents. The siege clearly established not only the bankruptcy of the NVA master plan, but also the ineptitude of their vaunted artillery. The press never saw this clearly… inexperienced as they were, they magnified the volume of enemy artillery rounds and disregarded the relative ineffectiveness of the enemy artillery.[111]

Later that month, he gave a presentation at CIA headquarters in Langley, Virginia to a group of staffers interested in his experiences. Meticulously uniformed, Baig entered and stood confidently at one end of a large conference table speaking for nearly an hour without the use of notes, often referring to several maps on an easel. Among those listening was George Allen, the CIA's Deputy Special Assistant for Vietnamese Affairs.

Like most Americans, Allen had been glued to TV images and news reports coming from Khe Sanh. But, unlike almost all of them, he had served three years in Indochina in the early 1950's, including seven weeks as the U.S. Army's chief intelligence analyst during the final days of Dien Bien Phu. Because of this, he understood what had occurred better than most in the room. "I was able to make a connection between what happened at Dien Bien Phu and what happened at Khe Sanh," he later said:

> That's one of the things that leads to my judgment about Khe Sanh having been 'the real thing.' He [Baig] presented a much different picture then one gets from reading what came out of Westmoreland's headquarters. All there [in the CIA briefing room] were awestruck by the brilliance of the concept, the scheme that he laid out, and how they had done all of this. [112]

Captain Baig was not shy about his role in saving the combat base from being captured, and described details of his creative countermeasures in a lengthy report to the Marine Corps Historical Branch. However, he could not, in good conscience, overlook the NVA's surprising tactical incompetency at crucial moments in the battle, their shocking lack of radio discipline, and a rigid adherence to their plan of battle over the course of the siege that left him with less guesswork to do as time went on. All this was part of what a disbelieving Baig was referring to when he wrote:

> I do not think that an account of the Khe Sanh siege will be complete without an explanation of the enemy state of mind, his battle tactics and his incredible behavior. They gave us a good fight; and, in the process, they destroyed themselves. A man [Giap] and a force [NVA] both known as past masters of guerrilla warfare, infiltration techniques and siege techniques, were finally revealed as stolid, rigid, inflexible and unbelievably foolish opponents.[113]

14
FLEETING GLORY

Baig would not speak of his own experiences in Vietnam with his family, other than to say, "The American public betrayed their servicemen while in battle."[114] But, before leaving Vietnam in late April, he did brief staff members from MACV and the ISC at Nakhon Phanom, Thailand on how he had utilized the top-secret system of sensors around Khe Sanh.

Over the previous ten weeks, Baig had orchestrated much of the over one hundred thousand tons of bombs dropped within a five-square-mile area around Khe Sanh (equivalent in destructive force to five Hiroshima-size atomic weapons), prompting General Westmoreland to describe it as "one of the heaviest and most concentrated displays of firepower in the history of war." Captain Baig had also targeted his attackers with a high percentage of the one hundred sixty thousand large-caliber artillery shells fired in defense of the base. For all this he was awarded the Legion of Merit, a highly unusual honor for a junior officer. The citation read in part:

> Captain Baig exhibited exceptional professionalism and imagination in planning a highly effective defense fire plan for the Khe Sanh Combat Base. Displaying keen analytic and organizational ability, he skillfully compared all such data received with other current intelligence information, compiling an overall estimate of the enemy's disposition that, when utilized for target designation, yielded a most effective tool for the assignment of targets for supporting arms.

After just three weeks on leave in the United States, Baig returned to South East Asia. On June 15, 1968, newly promoted to the rank of major, he was assigned to the U.S. Military Advisory Command-Thailand, although his official record of service also indicates he was attached to the U.S. State Department. Elated by his new duty station, he wrote in a letter to his mother: "At last, I can have my family with me in lovely Bangkok, and my office is next to the Prime Minister."[115]

This was not an idle boast. Thailand's head of state had taken a personal liking to this confident and sophisticated Marine major, as indicated in an even more unusual *second* Legion of Merit he would later receive:

> [Baig] was of extraordinary benefit to the Royal Thai Government and to the overall furtherance of United States intelligence efforts in Thailand. These contributions were in fact of such a nature as to prompt the Prime Minister of Thailand to officially request Major Baig's normal tour of duty extended.[116]

Now, with the official admiration of the Thai government and a new house being built for the family in Bangkok's embassy quarter, Baig once again felt the excitement of socializing in international, diplomatic circles, as he had earlier in life as the son of a respected general and Pakistani consul. Three years before, at Khe Sanh, he faced a challenge few junior officers in military history had, and resourcefully out-finessed the vaunted tactics employed by military icon General Vo Nguyen Giap in his spectacular victory over the French at Dien Bien Phu.

Having now marked his own place in history, Baig, with his adoring wife and daughter by his side, and his broad contributions and genius recognized by Legion of Merit honors, must have felt great satisfaction in what he had accomplished over a mere fourteen years since his enlistment as a private in the Marine Corps. There seemed to be no limit to what thirty-nine-year-old Major Munir Baig could accomplish in the future, if only given the chance.

But, that was not to be. While waiting for the construction of their home to be completed, the Baig's moved into the elegant, one-hundred-ten room Imperial Hotel. This upscale establishment catered primarily to foreign diplomats, well-heeled tourists and military officers and their families. At four a.m. on April 20, 1971, an undetected grease fire began in the kitchen of an all-night coffee shop on the ground floor of the hotel, a popular after-hours spot in the city. The fire quickly spread to a tank of natural gas used for cooking, touching off a thunderous explosion and sending flames roaring into the hotel reception area and up the main staircase. No alarm was sounded.

Pandemonium ensued as panicked guests groped their way through the smoke, searching in vain for outside fire escapes. Some discovered the emergency exit doors on the upper floor corridors were locked. Many jumped from windows causing serious injury or death. Others escaped by fashioning ropes from sheets. Several survived by making the perilous crawl across a makeshift ladder bridge to an adjacent building.

In the end, twenty-five people were killed, including six children. A UPI report stated that in some rooms "the bodies of parents and children were huddled together." [117] Among those found in such a tragic pose were Major Baig, his thirty-year-old wife Diane and nine-year-old daughter Cecile, all later determined by autopsy to have asphyxiated due to smoke inhalation.

When details about the tragedy were first released, and it was learned the hotel's exterior fire escapes had been removed, and some of the corridor exits had been secured with chains and padlocks, Baig's friends and family members speculated that he might have been the target of foul play, perhaps even assassination. However, a complete investigation concluded that the hotel's management had intentionally taken these unwise measures to foil a rash of night-time burglaries on the upper floors. The family's remains were buried in a single grave at Arlington National Cemetery on the morning of May 4, 1971, following a Catholic service at the Fort Myer Chapel.

Just a few months before his death, Baig had converted to Catholicism. His wife was Catholic and they had been married a decade earlier in a Catholic cathedral in Washington, D.C. Why he had chosen to convert remains a mystery, but his mother, and brother Taimur, believed this decision stemmed from the respect he had developed for chaplains ministering to the wounded and dying at Khe Sanh, particularly for his friend Father Walt Driscoll.[118]

Father Driscoll, a jovial, round-faced 40-year-old from Arlington, Massachusetts, often visited the FSCC room, snapping off an elaborate, quivering, palm-out British salute which Baig smartly returned to the amusement of us all. Between incoming artillery and mortar barrages, Driscoll spent his days crisscrossing the combat base aboard a sputtering, Japanese-made motor scooter. He had never ridden a motor bike before Khe Sanh, and so it amused many of us to see his grim-faced determination to stay attached to the handlebars as he bounced along the rutted dirt roads attending to the spiritual needs of the defenders.

When helicopters came to carry out the wounded, all denominations of chaplains would be there to assist. It was dangerous duty because NVA forward artillery observers on the high ground above the combat base could easily see what was transpiring and use it as an opportunity to kill or wound stretcher bearers (usually four to a stretcher) queuing up at the chopper doors to put the wounded onboard.

I volunteered to do this on two occasions and nothing compared to the seeming eternity of apprehension while standing in the deafening propeller wash unable to hear the mortar explosions. And yet, it was also a sublime "gut check" in knowing that—no matter what happened—I would not drop my corner of the stretcher containing such a vulnerable fellow human being. With the stretcher finally aboard, we would dash for cover. I always felt emotionally uplifted after that experience—a bit of my humanity restored after so many stultifying weeks of endless bombardment waiting for my turn on the stretcher, or in a body bag.

These chaplains took such risks every day and suffered for it. On February 22, Father Driscoll's fellow Catholic chaplain, Lieutenant Raymond R. Brett of Collingdale, Pennsylvania, was killed when an enemy rocket exploded amid wounded men he was attending to on the runway. A few days later, Father Driscoll was badly injured in the upper back by mortar shrapnel. He would survive, but remain a paraplegic for the remainder of his life. Just before his injury, he told war correspondent Peter Arnett: "Two square miles and six thousand souls. Not much of a parish back home. But I'm here and I'll stay. I think they need me."[119] It is little wonder Baig was so taken with such examples of duty and courage.

At the family's funeral service in Arlington, Munir's father, mother and brother were surprised at the number of distinguished dignitaries in attendance. "We were absolutely flabbergasted," Taimur later said, "that they would come out for the funeral of a major."[120] Among them were an admiral and several generals, including Robert Cushman, now Deputy Director of the CIA and Rathvon Tompkins. Both men had directly commanded Baig in South Vietnam, knew him well, and held him in the highest esteem. Later that day, Juliette was told that General Tompkins, a tough and highly decorated veteran of ferocious Second World War fighting on Guadalcanal and Tarawa, broke into tears upon learning of Baig's death.

The family was then surprised to learn that Major Baig had been involved in highly classified clandestine intelligence work in Laos. "The information slipped out at a luncheon in the military club given us by a Marine major," Osman recalled, "who mentioned what an authentic Laotian Munir looked like once made-up and dressed in special clothes with his French accent."[121] Upon asking why his son was in Laos, Osman was told only that he was carrying out special missions for President Nixon directed through National Security Adviser Henry Kissinger. "As a life-long diplomat," Osman said, "I shut up!"

The family was then invited to dinner at the home of Marine Corps Commandant General Leonard F. Chapman, who told Major Baig's parents: "You have lost a son, but we have lost a special Marine."[122]

Just a month later, on June 5, 1971, the NVA overran the American electronic surveillance station on Hill 950—the last outpost at Khe Sanh.

Baig family resting place at Arlington National Cemetery. Front and reverse of the same grave marker. (*National Archives and Records Administration*)

The fort at Bijapur, circa 1870, Its likeness was on the Baig family crest. (Can Stock Photo, Inc.)

Sixteenth-century Mughal Empire "Gunpowder Prince" and artillerymen. Note the khukri sword on his hip, similar to one worn by Captain Munir Baig at Khe Sanh four hundred years later. *(Illustration by Byam Shaw in "The Adventures of Akbar" by Flora Annie Steel (London: William Heinemann, 1913).*

15
SHADOW WARRIOR

Baig's secret work in the war-torn Kingdom of Laos remains a mystery. Bob Coolidge, his close friend and fellow intelligence officer at Khe Sanh, later stated that, "Harry was specifically recruited for that job, to do that [assignment] in Laos."[123] This was likely due to his practical experience in these kinds of clandestine activities from his counterintelligence activities along the DMZ in 1963, interrogating prisoners, cultivating informants and building a spy network into North Vietnam.

His activities in Laos undoubtedly related to the CIA's decade-long paramilitary operation there, directing native units against Pathet Lao communists. The character of that conflict changed in 1968 when the NVA, impatient with the progress of the Pathet Lao, increased their combat forces in the country. By mid-March, and concurrent with the siege of Khe Sanh just across the border; NVA armored forces captured the Royal Laotian Army camp at Ban Houie San, overran a key navigational facility that was used by the U.S. Air Force for bombing North Vietnam; and threatened to push the American-friendly forces of the Hmong ethnic group out of their mountaintop strongholds surrounding the Plain of Jars in the north. In addition, about forty thousand NVA troops remained engaged in protecting supplies moving down the Ho Chi Minh Trail.

To counter this, the U.S. increased the use of airpower to such a level that Laos would ultimately be pounded by two and one half million tons of bombs—more than what then dropped in the Second World War on

Germany and Japan combined—making Laos, per capita, the most heavily bombed nation in history.

Timothy Castle is a widely acknowledged expert on the CIA's secret war in Laos, and author of the book *At War in The Shadow of Vietnam*. Castle served two tours in Southeast Asia during the Vietnam War and later had a career with the CIA. He has traveled to Laos frequently in recent years as a researcher and senior Department of Defense POW/MIA investigator, and is currently a senior researcher at the CIA Center for the Study of Intelligence.

In 2016, Castle speculated on the bits of information Baig's family and friends had gathered about his activities in Laos: "It's very likely that Major Baig was assigned not to the traditional Military Assistance Advisory Group working with the Joint United States Military Advisory Group Thailand, but rather the covert Deputy Chief, Joint United States Military Advisory Group Thailand (DEPCHIEF)" which served to expedite the supply needs of the Royal Lao Army fighting under Department of Defense and CIA direction.[124]

The CIA ran most of the ground war in Laos from Udorn in Thailand as part of a strategy to appear in compliance with Geneva Accords honoring the neutrality of Laos. This location gave the Agency access, not only to the DEPCHIEF and the headquarters of the Thai "volunteers" in Laos, trained and paid by the CIA; but, also the use of aircraft, including the Agency's own Air America, and those commanded by the U.S. Seventh Air Force, Thirteenth Air Force Headquarters (7/13th AF).

Castle further surmised that it was possible, given Baig's background in conducting the air war at Khe Sanh, that he could have been advising the targeting officers at 7/13th AF: "Although, I suspect they might have been reluctant, as a matter of professional pride, to take advice from him." He also may have been asked to provide his expertise to either the CIA staff in the 4802nd Joint Liaison Detachment at Udorn, or their station in the Laotian capital of Vientiane.

The Vientiane CIA station would have presented Baig with an unusually complicated situation as it was run under the intense supervision of the U.S. Secretary of State's ambassador. Because bombing in Laos was an extremely sensitive, politically volatile, situation, the White House was deeply involved in picking targets, making Baig's input in such a selection largely process superfluous.

Thai battalions now comprised a sizable share of the forces fighting the NVA in Laos and soon had some success in regaining lost territory and establishing an effective network of artillery strongpoints.

From Baig's admittedly close professional association with the Royal Thai Army's military intelligence personnel, and his own expertise in the use of artillery, it might seem logical to assume that he was stationed with the Thai volunteer battalions in Laos, possibly helping establish that network of artillery strongpoints. However, since CIA paramilitary officers already advised these Thai forces, it is doubtful Baig was working with them.

None of these possibilities explain why Baig would have been wearing Lao garb and speaking French, as his family was told at his funeral. Castle conjectured that this suggested Baig was with the Royal Lao army in the southern part of the country, rather than at Udorn, Vientiane or with Hmong fighters in the north.

Thomas L. Ahern Jr., a renowned CIA operations officer for more than thirty years, offers a tantalizing possibility about what Baig may have been doing in Laos in early 1971. In his book *Undercover Armies, CIA and Surrogate Warfare in Laos,* Ahern describes how Robert Cushman, Deputy Director of the CIA, bemoaned to the Nixon White House that friendly indigenous forces were unsuccessful in creating a significant-enough diversion in the west to split NVA forces in fending off Operation Lam Son 719. This operation involved thousands of South Vietnamese troops, with U.S. supporting arms, striking out at the Ho Chi Minh Trail from the Khe Sanh Combat Base, briefly reopened for this purpose from January through March 1971.

Cushman believed the problem was due to the CIA's lack of the artillery expertise needed to keep these forces moving forward under a protective umbrella from their firebases.[125] As mentioned previously, Cushman had been a Marine lieutenant general in 1967, commanding the Third Marine Amphibious Force in South Vietnam. There, he had personally known Baig, and greatly respected what the captain had already accomplished with his dual expertise in artillery and counterintelligence.

If this were the case, Baig may have been in southern Laos, near Tchepone, about forty miles west of his old "home" at Khe Sanh, participating in Operation Silver Buckle. The operation was initiated in January 1971 as a planned diversion for Lam Son 719. Silver Buckle was conducted largely by CIA-sponsored Royal Lao guerrilla battalions, assembled under a unit with the French name *Groupement Mobile 30*. Here Baig would have easily assimilated in Lao clothing and speaking excellent French. Also, Silver Buckle happened to be the first time the CIA would arrange air support with the U.S. Air Force well in advance of an operation, for which Baig had ample expertise. In early February, Silver Buckle ended in full retreat after two NVA infantry regiments, backed by tanks, antiaircraft guns and artillery, overran a *Groupement Mobile 30* camp.

Ahern's account of Deputy Director Cushman's dilemma, as described in *Undercover Armies*, seemed, finally, to have led me to an answer about the nature of Major Baig's clandestine work in Laos. However, the text immediately following that passage in the book is heavily censored for security reasons.

Frustrated by the possibility of getting so close, and coming up with nothing, I submitted a Freedom of Information Act request to the CIA for any documents they have indicating a connection between the Agency and Baig. In addition, I specifically requested that those expurgated segments in *Undercover Armies* be reclassified and made available.

In January 2018, I received a reply by mail from the CIA's information and privacy coordinator, advising me that "after conducting a search reasonably calculated to uncover all relevant documents, we did not locate any responsive records that would reveal an openly acknowledged CIA affiliation with the subject [Baig]."

Regarding my request to have certain parts of *Undercover Armies* reclassified:

> To the extent that your request also seeks records that would reveal a classified association between the CIA and the subject, if any exist, we can neither confirm nor deny having such records. If a classified association between the subject and this organization were to exist, records

revealing such a relationship would be properly classified and required continued safeguards against unauthorized disclosure. [126]

While this reply appears somewhat opaque, it does seem to concede one important point: The Agency will not, or cannot, deny such an association existed.

What *can* be documented as relevant, was Baig's relationship with many at the highest levels of the military and government. As a captain (and later as a major), he was awarded the prestigious Legion of Merit. This honor is bestowed upon U.S. military personnel, and political figures of foreign governments, for exceptionally meritorious conduct in the performance of outstanding services and achievements. In the Marine Corps, it is rarely awarded to ranks below colonel. Authority to nominate for the Legion of Merit is reserved for generals only; or as civilians, for the level of Assistant Secretary of Defense and up, including the president. Baig's second Legion of Merit, as described previously, seems to have been inspired by admiration from the Prime Minister of Thailand—highly unusual for anyone, let alone a lower-ranking officer.

In May 1971, CIA Deputy Director Cushman was among a bevy of dignitaries, including several other generals and an admiral, who attended Baig's funeral at Arlington Cemetery. This immediately raised eyebrows about why so many significant representatives of Washington's military and intelligence communities were attending the funeral of an otherwise little-known Marine Corps major. One answer lies in the likelihood that Major Baig was involved in some highly-classified, clandestine activities coordinated between the Department of Defense and CIA.

* * *

Despite his extraordinary life and accomplishments, Munir Baig lived and died in relative obscurity. I would not learn of his death until thirty years later in the mid-1990s, and then only by chance while chatting with a neighbor who had been a Marine intelligence officer in Vietnam and knew Baig by reputation. It would not be until improvements in the search capabilities of the Internet, and later research by Khe Sanh historian Reverend Ray W. Stubbe, that I would gather the grim details.

In talking with my neighbor that day, I suddenly remembered how I had felt so much a part of the extraordinary atmosphere in the FSCC room of the Khe Sanh command bunker. For about a year after my return to civilian life, I had a recurring dream of being called back to join that group of men—Baig, Hennelly, Hudson, Steen and the others—at an unidentifiable dreamland location, other than Khe Sanh, which was under siege and required our expertise. In the dream, I could feel unmistakable contentment at the thought of rejoining them—as if it were the only natural place I belonged.

About ten years later, in June 2004, I wrote a letter to famed photojournalist David Douglas Duncan asking permission to reprint some of his photos in my book *A Patch of Ground*. Eighty-year-old David responded by telephone from his home in the south of France, opening the conversion with a gruff: "So you didn't get your ass shot off at Khe Sanh, huh?"

He had photographed wars since the early 1940s, mostly for LIFE magazine, and I recalled seeing him in the command center bunker at Khe Sanh in February 1968. In his subsequent book, *War Without Heroes*, Duncan included a photo he had taken of Baig, who he described in the book as "a renegade Pakistani-Mongol-turned-Marine" and a "Mad Mongol."[127]

David told me that after publication of the book, he received a letter from Baig's father, Osman, asking that David respect his recently deceased son's memory by removing those references; and threatened to use his diplomatic influence to have future printings of the books stopped if he refused. David realized the elder Baig had no idea how instrumental his son had been in saving thousands of American lives during that battle, and so sent him more information about Captain Baig's work at Khe Sanh. Osman recontacted David, and with great emotion said, "Thank you for giving me back my son." After telling me this story, David asked: "Can you imagine how powerful a man he was?" What privilege Baig grew up in?"

Over the course of his renowned, professional life, David came to know countless celebrities in the arts and athletics, and numerous world political and military leaders. So, when he asked me those two rhetorical questions, I sensed that he had been surprised by Osman's unconcealed expression of love for his son; coming, as it did from such a significant "Old World" military leader and accomplished international diplomat with a reputation for public composure.

For his wife Juliette, the deaths of her son, daughter-in-law and granddaughter were devastating. She later recalled a day in 1937 when she took then-five-year-old Munir to a monument in London called the Cenotaph, honoring Britain's fallen soldiers from the First World War. After studying the memorial for some time, the little boy looked up at her and said "But, mommy, I will not get killed when I go to war."[128]

It was no consolation to this grieving mother that he technically kept his word, surviving an unprecedented level of mortal danger in South Vietnam and Laos.

16
THE GUNPOWDER PRINCE

Chief among the mysteries that remain unanswered about Major Munir Baig is: Who was this complex character? Though serving in the American military with great pride, Baig was physically present on U.S. soil less than ten of his nearly forty years of life. He seemed to have preferred living abroad; the last three and a half years of his life, with the exception a three-week visit to Washington, D.C., were spent in Southeast Asia.

Much of the privileged life to which he had been born was undone after postcolonial independence for India and Pakistan. His father's choice to become a Pakistani diplomat, and the subsequent breakdown of relations between Britain and Pakistan, cost Munir a legacy appointment to Sandhurst and a bright career following in his Osman's footsteps as an officer in the British army. "He always wanted to be a soldier," his brother Taimur said. "I guess because of dad."[129]

Joining the Marine Corps as an enlisted recruit did not appear to have dashed Baig's aristocratic spirit. Upon graduation from Officer Candidates School three years later, he married the daughter of a French nobleman whose family roots went back centuries to Knight Crusaders.

Taimur, who, despite having a degree from Harvard, chose to enter the U.S. Army, also as an enlisted man, and later enjoyed a successful career as an executive with the World Bank, recalled that his brother "was quite eccentric." In the early-1960s, Taimur said, Munir "fancied himself as an English country gentleman and wandered around in jodhpurs and his cravat, which, of course, didn't go down too well with Americans."[130]

During Baig's time in 1964 at El Toro Marine Corps Air Station in California, his friend Bob Coolidge visited the Baig home frequently, recalling Munir's impeccable tailor-made civilian wardrobe. This included several smoking jackets, a silk garment traditionally reserved for evening wear in the comfort of one's aristocratic English estate. Home life, Coolidge said, typically ran on a schedule of Baig returning home from work and changing clothes, after which three-year-old daughter Cecile appeared in the living room to recite what she had learned that day. She was then sent off to bed at 8 p.m. when Munir and Diane sat down to dinner together. "Harry," Coolidge said "was very British."

Yet, at the same time, Baig seemed to be experiencing a crisis of identity at odds with this British persona. His friend, Major Bill Bates, recalled that, in 1966, when the two first met at Amphibious Warfare School in Virginia, the staff asked them to reveal some information about themselves, particularly any family connection to the military. Baig immediately wrote that he was heir to "a seven-hundred-year-old family of warriors." Later in Vietnam, when Bates visited Baig at his artillery battery compound near Phu Bai, he was amused to see the Baig family ancestral flag conspicuously flying atop a watch tower. [131]

At Khe Sanh, we all noticed a ring Captain Baig wore bearing that same family crest: two Mughal curved swords, called a talwar, crossing one another over a representation of the impressive arched gate of the old Bijapur fort, with its ornate parapets and crenellations, considered among the finest architecture in India.

Baig's rootlessness from years living in colonial India, then France, England, Canada, the United States, South Vietnam, Laos and Thailand, seemed to have kept him closely tied to a distant identification with the great Mughal Empire in central Asia and northern India.

This cherished historical link, coupled with the imaginative artillery techniques Baig devised to save the Khe Sanh Combat Base, would take on a strangely fated connection to his ancestor Babur, another military adventurer of remarkable genius, and founder of the Mughal Empire. The Mughal, along with the Ottoman and Safavid, are referred to by historians as the *Islamic gunpowder empires,* derived from the considerable success their armies had devising creative improvements in the use of newly developing cannon and musket technology. Of the three, the Mughal

Empire would become the largest, by far, ruling well over one hundred million people.

A prodigy by the time he became emperor at age twelve, Babur applied his exceptional historical awareness and keen intellect to master the art of field artillery. His innovative tactical schemes would include cavalry flanking formations used to push attacking forces into the range of his artillery, and a system of ropes and wheels that allowed heavy cannons to be rapidly traversed onto new targets of opportunity. At the First Battle of Panipat in 1526, Babur's forces were heavily outnumbered by his Afghan and Rajput adversaries, both of whom lacked gunpowder weapons and relied on archaic tactics, including the use of war elephants. Babur's victory was so astonishing that few opponents would ever again choose to meet Mughal princes in pitched battle.

The Baigs had fought at Panipat that day and remained gunpowder princes of the empire. As a direct descendant, Captain Munir Baig would engage in similar artillery artistry four hundred fifty years later, on another Asian battlefield. Like Babur, he was ever mindful of the historical imperatives that had formed his adversary's tactics and the inflexibility with which they would carry them out in battle. Confident in this knowledge, Baig devised his own revolutionary methods, using the weapons available to him, to defeat another numerically superior force.

In December 1968, Major Baig provided the Marine Corps Historical Branch with details of his activities during the siege of Khe Sanh. Ever cognizant of his place in history, he began this narrative by apologizing in advance for sounding "bombastic or boastful," then offered, as an excuse for doing just that, a quote from the ancient Roman poet Virgil: "These things I saw, and a part of them I was."

He then reveled in his success against the legendary Giap, derisively acknowledging that the architect of the sensational 1954 victory at Dien Bien Phu could have easily defeated the Americans at Khe Sanh, had he done his homework:

> Some of the credit must go to General Giap. Our experience during the 77 days, legitimately raises the question, 'Who besieged whom?' For a man, who, in civil life was alleged to have been a teacher of mathematics, General Giap had

not studied his Vauban very closely. Had he profited from the teachings of the 18th century French master of siege craft, Giap could have caught us in the 'toils on Euclid' to our possible discomfort. [132]

That quaint expression comes from a time of groundbreaking developments in siege tactics refined by the Marquis de Vauban, the foremost military engineer of his age, famed for his skill in both constructing fortifications and breaking into them. His methods would become the dominant model for siegecraft and fortress design into the twentieth century. These revolutionary techniques included digging trenches parallel to the walls of a defensive fortification, often in a zig-zag pattern, making them comparatively safe from defensive artillery. Vauban also advanced the use of precisely angled, ricocheting artillery fire (think of a "bank shot" in billiards) to inflict maximum damage in the process of breaching battlements.

Vauban's early education, grounded in mathematics, shaped his siege techniques with such geometric precision that progress could be calculated, one step following another, until a defending commander, now caught in these "toils of Euclid,"[133] had only two grim alternatives—surrender or face a final breaching and the inevitable vengeful consequences.

This was the dilemma that confronted Mirza Imam Ali Baig in the mid-nineteenth century when he chose to surrender the fort at Bijapur to the British—a stain on the honor of this fiercely proud clan—that was now expunged one hundred twenty years later by his great-grandson's successful defense of "his" fort at Khe Sanh. Juliette Baig agreed: "Ali Baig's position at Bijapur was hereditary in the family, and Munir assumed it was still his—but for the British invasion!"[134]

Her husband, Osman, shared this notion and was also a believer in the ability to communicate with the spirits of his ancestors. Munir greatly admired his father, and we can only speculate whether he attended such séances with him as a young man. If so, it would have undoubtedly created a powerful connection to his roots and his responsibility in caring for the family honor.

The CIA's George Allen later said: "I had agonized so long over how nobody in Vietnam seemed to be drawing on all the stuff that we'd accumulated during the French war, and was so pleased that here was a guy who did—and entirely on his own initiative."[135] Yet, Baig had taken it a step further, seeking to absorb the thought processes of his adversaries, not just by reading everything they wrote and said in public, but also learning what they had read as students and young revolutionaries, sculpting their methods. General Giap, for example, was a great admirer Sun Tzu's philosophy, Napoleon's generalship, and the tactical practicalities so eloquently described in T. E. Lawrence's *Seven Pillars of Wisdom*.

Ultimately, the fate of Khe Sanh hinged on this self-initiative by Captain Baig, and the seemingly absurd fact that he came to those remote mountains with an awareness of his own personal destiny, an old family score to settle, and a few well-thumbed volumes of antiquated British, French and Vietnamese military history.

David Douglas Duncan, who captured some of the most gripping and iconic photos of war in the twentieth century, would end his thirty-year career as a combat photographer at Khe Sanh. David later wrote that, of all the Marines holding Khe Sanh against the NVA, none was more important to their survival than Baig: "It was the biggest chess game played in Vietnam, with Giap matched against a master [Baig] who anticipated his every move."[136]

Captain Kent Steen, who worked as closely with Baig as anyone did, and was "more aware than most how near [tenuous] a thing our survival was,"[137] later wrote: "With the perspective of age, I realize the Marine Corps attracts strongly put together people, but Harry was clearly of another genius. The rest of us were probably interchangeable—Harry was one of a kind."[138]

The End

BIBLIOGRAPHY

Books

Thomas L. Ahern Jr., *Undercover Armies CIA and Surrogate Warfare in Laos*, (Center for the Study of Intelligence, 2006)

Michael Archer, *A Patch of Ground: Khe Sanh Remembered*, (Hellgate Press, 2005)

Bao Ninh, *The Sorrow of War* (London: Secker & Warburg 1993)

William Blum, *Killing Hope: U.S. Military and CIA Interventions Since World War II* (Zed Books, 2003)

Michael Beschloss, *Reaching for Glory: Lyndon Johnson's Secret White House Tapes, 1964-1965* (Simon & Schuster; Reprint edition 2002)

Robert Coram, *Brute: The Life of Victor Krulak, U.S. Marine* (Little, Brown and Company; 1st ed., 2010)

Peer DeSilva, *Sub Rosa: The CIA and the Uses of Intelligence* (New York: Times Books, 1978)

General Dong Si Nguyen, *The Trans-Truong Son Route* (The GIOI Publishers, 2005)

Bernard Fall, *Street Without Joy*, (Mechanicsburg, PA: Stackpole Books 1994)

Ann Finkbeiner, *The Jasons: The Secret History of Science's Postwar Elite*, (Viking Penguin, NYC, 2006)

Harold P. Ford, *Revisiting Vietnam: Thoughts Engendered by Robert McNamara's In Retrospect*, https://www.cia.gov/library/center-for-the-study-of-intelligence/csi-publications/csi-studies/studies/96unclass/ford.htmsigma

David Halberstam, *Ho*, (New York, Random House, 1971)

George C. Herring, *America's Longest War: The United States and Vietnam 1950-1975*, (McGraw-Hill 2002)

Brigadier General Hoang Dan and Captain Hung Dat, *Highway 9—Khe Sanh Offensive Campaign: Spring and Summer 1968*, Vietnam Institute of Military History, Hanoi, 1987)

Hoang Ngoc Lung, *The General Offensives of 1968-69*. McLean VA: General Research Corporation (1978)

Gregg Jones, *Last Stand at Khe Sanh: The U.S. Marines' Finest Hour in Vietnam* (Da Capo Press, 2013)

Victor H. Krulak, *First to Fight: An Inside View of the U.S. Marine Corps* (Naval Institute Press, Annapolis, MD, 1999)

Lanning, Michael & Cragg Dan, *Inside the VC and NVA: The Story of North Vietnams' Armed Forces* (Texas A&M University Press, 2008)

Lien-Hang T. Nguyen, *Hanoi's War: An International History of the War for Peace in Vietnam* (University of North Carolina Press, 2012)

Edward F. Murphy, *The Hill Fights: The First Battle of Khe Sanh* (New York: Ballantine Books, 2003).

Bernard C. Nalty, *Air Power and the Fight for Khe Sanh* (Office of Air Force History, United States Air Force, Washington, D.C., 1986)

Robert Pisor, *The End of the Line: The Siege of Khe Sanh* (Ballantine Books, 1983)

John Prados and Ray W. Stubbe, *Valley of Decision: The Siege of Khe Sanh* (Annapolis MD: Naval Institute Press, 1991)

Neil Sheehan, *A Bright Shining Lie: John Paul Vann and America in Vietnam* (New York: Random House, 1988)

Moyers S. Shore III, *The Battle for Khe Sanh*, (History and Museums Division, Headquarters, U.S. Marine Corps, Washington, D.C., 1969)

Jack Shulimson, U.S. *Marines in Vietnam: The Defining Year 1968* (History & Museums Division, Headquarters U.S. Marine Corps Washington, D.C. 1997)

Lewis Sorley, *A Better War: The Unexamined Victories and Final Tragedy of America's Last Year in Vietnam*, (Boston: Harcourt, Inc., 1999)

Lewis Sorley, *Westmoreland: The General Who Lost Vietnam* (Boston: Houghton Mifflin Harcourt 2011)

Ronald Spector, *After Tet: The Bloodiest Year in Vietnam* (New York: Free Press 1992)

Ray W. Stubbe, *Battalion of Kings: A Tribute to Our Fallen Brothers Who Died Because of the Battlefield of Khe Sanh, Vietnam*, 1st ed. (Wauwatosa, WI: Khe Sanh Veterans, 2005)

— *B5-T8 in 48 QXD: The Secret Official History of the North Vietnamese Army of the Siege at Khe Sanh, Vietnam, Spring, 1968* (Wauwatosa, WI: Khe Sanh Veterans, 2006)

— *Pebbles in My Boots Vol. 2*, (Wauwatosa, WI, 2011)

— *Pebbles in My Boots Vol. 3*, (Wauwatosa, WI, 2014)

William C. Westmoreland, *A Soldier Reports*, (New York: Doubleday, 1976)

Articles & Studies, Films

Peter Brush, "*The Withdrawal from Khe Sanh.*" http://www.vwam.com/client/contentclient.php?intIdContent=22

Peter Brush, *The Unexploited Vulnerability of the Marines at Khe Sanh*, (Vietnam Magazine, August, 1997) pp.58-60.

Lieutenant General John A. Chaisson, USMC, Historical Center, Oral history, 1975

Major Norman L. Cooling, *Hue City, 1968: Winning A Battle While Losing A War*, 2001 https://www.mca-marines.org/gazette/hue-city-1968-winning-battle-while-losing-war

George Magazine, "A Special Interview with General William Westmoreland," November 1998

William Head, *Bloodshed and Bitterness: The Battle for Khe Sanh, Diversion or a Second Dien Bien Phu?* www.virginiareviewofasianstudies.com.

Nguyen Duc Huy, *Major General Nguyen Duc Huy: A Life in the Military, Second Edition, with Additions and Corrections,* (People's Army Publishing House, Hanoi, 2011), translated by Merle L. Pribbenow.

People's Army newspaper, Lieutenant General Dang Kinh, "The Tri-Thien-Hue Battlefield (Installment 1)," 27 Jan 2008, translated by Merle Pribbenow. *http://www.qdnd.vn/qdnd/baongay.psks.phongsu.28802.qdnd.*

Marc Levy, "An Interview with Bao Ninh: Part One," *The Veteran: Magazine of the Vietnam Veterans Against the War* (Fall/ Winter 1999).

Colonel D.E. Lownds, taped historical interview (debriefing), 29 July 1968, Headquarters Fleet Marine Force, Pacific.

James I. Marino, *Strategic Crossroads at Khe Sanh*, VIETNAM magazine, December 1999.

Military Institute of Vietnam, translated by Merle Pribbenow, *Victory in Vietnam* (Lawrence, Kansas: University of Kansas Press, 2002).

John Prados, *Khe Sanh: The Other Side of The Hill*, The VVA Veteran, July-August 2007.

Stubbe, Ray W., *Khe Sanh and The Mongol Prince*, (unpublished manuscript, 2002).

TIME, "The Red Napoleon" June 17, 1966.

CHAPTER NOTES

1. Juliette Baig, transcript of interview with Ray W. Stubbe, August 15, 2000, Wisconsin Veterans Museum, Madison Wisconsin.

2. *Eminent Mussulmans*, (G.A. Natesan & Company, Madras) p. 434.

3. Her son's (Taimur) Virginia marriage license in July 1965 shows Juliette's maiden name as "Mulkie."

4. Ray W. Stubbe, *Battalion of Kings: A Tribute to Our Fallen Brothers Who Died Because of the Battlefield of Khe Sanh, Vietnam, First* ed. (Wauwatosa, WI: Khe Sanh Veterans, 2005), p. 13.

5. Krulak, *First to Fight,* (Annapolis: Naval Institute Press, 1999) p. 208.

6. *Ibid.*, p. 199. Krulak proved to be correct. By 1972, the allies had managed to reduce the enemy manpower by only 25 percent at a cost of over 220,000 U.S. and South Vietnamese dead.

7. *Ibid.*, p. 210.

8. William Head, *Bloodshed and Bitterness: The Battle for Khe Sanh, Diversion or a Second Dien Bien Phu?* www.virginiareviewofasianstudies.com.

9. William C. Westmoreland, *A Soldier Reports* (New York City: Doubleday, 1976), p. 339.

10. Lewis Sorley, *Westmoreland: The General Who Lost Vietnam* (Boston: Houghton Mifflin Harcourt, 2011), p. 175.

11. Ray W. Stubbe, *B5-T8 in 48 QXD, The Secret Official History of the North Vietnamese Army of the Siege at Khe Sanh, Vietnam, Spring, 1968* (Khe Sanh Veterans, Inc. Wauwatosa, WI 2006), translations by Sedgwick D. Tourison, Jr. and Robert J. DeStatte, p. 16.

12. "Ali" is a surname passed along to males in the Baig family implying an elevated social or religious status, but commonly dropped for the sake of brevity.

13. Lady Baig would remain living in London until the German bombing in 1940, when she returned to India.

14. Taimur Baig, transcript of interview with Ray W. Stubbe, November 22, 2000, Wisconsin Veterans Museum, Madison Wisconsin.

15. Juliette Baig, *op. cit.*, August 15, 2000.

16. *Ibid.*

17. *Ibid.*

18. Stubbe, Ray W., *Khe Sanh and The Mongol Prince*, (unpublished manuscript, 2002), p. 11. NOTE: Author Stubbe's research materials, interview transcripts, etc. are catalogued and available at the Wisconsin Veterans Museum, Madison, Wisconsin.

19. Juliette Baig interview, *op. cit.*

20. https://marines.togetherweserved.com/usmc/servlet/tws.webapp.WebApp?cmd=ShadowBoxProfile&type=Person&ID=112866.

21. Stubbe, *Mongol Prince, op. cit.*, p. 12.

22. *New York Times,* Obituary, June 7, 1964.

23. William Blum, *Killing Hope: U.S. Military and CIA Interventions Since World War II* (Zed Books, 2003), p.142.

24. Declassified memorandum December 23, 1968 from Major Mirza Munir Baig, Headquarters, United States Military Assistance Command, Thailand, Joint United States Military Advisory Group, Thailand to Headquarters USMC, Historical Records Branch, G-3 Division.

25. Major William Bates interview with author, September 22, 2016.

26. *Ibid.*

27. The distinctive blade-form of the khukri short sword, which Baig wore on his hip each day at Khe Sanh, was introduced into the subcontinent by the Macedonian army of Alexander the Great in the in the fourth century B.C.E. The design was soon adopted by ancient tribes throughout the Himalayas, as a combination of agricultural tool and fearsome weapon for close-in "hand-to-hand" fighting.

28. Jack Shulimson, *U.S. Marines in Vietnam: The Defining Year 1968* (History & Museums Division, Headquarters U.S. Marine Corps Washington, D.C., 1997), p. 64.

29. Mark A. Swearengen, unpublished memoir, March 10, 2010.

30. John Prados, *Khe Sanh: The Other Side of the Hill,* The VVA Veteran, Jul-Aug 2007, p. 4.

31. Military Institute of Vietnam, translated by Merle Pribbenow, *Victory in Vietnam* (Lawrence Kansas: University of Kansas Press, 2002), p. 216.

32. Jerry Hudson, transcript of interview with Ray W. Stubbe, May 4, 1990, Wisconsin Veterans Museum, Madison, Wisconsin.

33. Institute for Defense Analyses-Jason Division, *Air-supported Anti-infiltration Barrier,* August 1966.

34. Ann Finkbeiner, *The Jasons: The Secret History of Science's Postwar Elite,* (Viking Penguin, NYC, 2006)

35. Baig interview, April 24, 1968, *op. cit*

36. Captain Mirza M. Baig interview with the Military Assistance Command Science Advisor (MACSA), April 24, 1968.

37. Baig memo, December 23, 1968, *op. cit.*

38. Baig interview, *op. cit.*

39. *Ibid.*

40. *Ibid.*

41. *Ibid.*

42. Institute for Defense Analyses-Jason Division, *Tactical Nuclear Weapons in Southeast Asia,* March 1967.

43. *Ibid.*

44. Lien-Hang T. Nguyen, *Hanoi's War: An International History of the War for Peace in Vietnam* (University of North Carolina Press, 2012), p. 309.

45. James I. Marino, *Strategic Crossroads at Khe Sanh, VIETNAM* magazine, December 1999.

46. Interview with Major General Nguyen Duc Huy
http://www.historynet.com/interviews-with-a-top-north-vietnam-army-general-and-two-former-soldiers.htm

47. Baig memo, *op. cit.*

48. *Ibid.*

49. *Ibid.*

50. Nguyen Duc Huy, *Major General Nguyen Duc Huy: A Life in the Military,* Second Edition, with Additions and Corrections, (People's Army Publishing House, Hanoi, 2011), translated by Merle L. Pribbenow, p. 69.

51. *Ibid.*

52. Colonel William H. Dabney, USMC (Ret.), Interviewed by Jim Dietrich, *Cold War Oral History Project, Center for Military History and Strategic Analysis* (Virginia Military Institute Archives, Military Oral History Collection), September 8, 2005.

53. The People's Republic of China would claim that they had sent hundreds of thousands of their soldiers to North Vietnam during the war against the Americans, most to assist in noncombatant roles to free up North Vietnamese soldiers to fight in the south.

54. Author's nickname at the time from having fought alongside the Bru tribe of Montagnards in Khe Sanh village earlier that year.

55. Baig memo, *op. cit.*

56. Baig memo, *op. cit.*

57. *Ibid.*

58. *Ibid.*

59. Walter O. Driscoll, letter to Ray W. Stubbe, December 14, 2000, Wisconsin Veterans Museum, Madison, Wisconsin.

60. Swearengen, memoir, *op. cit.*, March 19, 2010.

61. Mark Swearengen, transcript of interview with Ray W. Stubbe, January 17, 1997, Wisconsin Veterans Museum, Madison, Wisconsin.

62. Bernard Cole, letter to Ray W. Stubbe, May 25, 2000, Wisconsin Veterans Museum, Madison, Wisconsin.

63. Hudson, May 4, 1990, *op. cit.*

64. Kent Steen, letter to Ray W. Stubbe, January 18, 2001, Wisconsin Veterans Museum, Madison, Wisconsin.

65. Cole, May 25, 2000, *op. cit.*

66 . Stubbe, *B5-T8, op. cit.,* p.*80*

67. *Ibid.,* p.79.

68. http://www.air-america.org/images/docs/rgj_moore_ls85.pdf
On Jan. 11, 1968, ten days before the siege of Khe Sanh began, North Vietnamese pilots flying two Russian-built "Colt" biplanes attacked a secret American radar base in northern Laos. Neither aircraft were equipped with missiles and machine guns, instead both had been modified to carry mortar shells which were dropped through holes cut in the belly of the aircraft. Air America pilot Ted Moore, flying a UH-1 (Huey) helicopter on a routine resupply mission to the radar station, and unequipped with missiles and machine guns, chased the two biplanes while Glen Woods, his flight engineer, fired an AK-47 rifle from the side door. One of the planes caught fire and crashed. The other flew beneath the helicopter and slammed into a mountainside. "It blew me away to see biplanes," Moore later said. "It was like we traveled back in time to World War I Europe."

69. *Analysis of the Khe Sanh Battle* prepared for MACV, April 5, 1968, p.87, noted that intelligence from many sources indicated conclusively that the North Vietnamese had planned a massive ground attack against the base. The attack was to have been supported by armor and artillery. Having to push up the attack date to January 20 from early February, and losses inflicted on the enemy in the opening days of the attack, were of sufficient magnitude to cause the enemy to abandon this plan.

70. Baig memo, *op. cit.*

71. *Ibid.*

72. Stubbe, *B5-T8, op. cit.*

73. John Prados and Ray W. Stubbe, *Valley of Decision: The Siege of Khe Sanh* (Annapolis MD: Naval Institute Press, 1991), p. 406.

74. Prados and Stubbe, *Valley of Decision, op.cit.*, p.407.

75. *The New York Times*, February 12, 1968.

76. Prados and Stubbe, *Valley of Decision, op.cit.*, p.409.

77. Colonel D.E. Lownds, taped historical interview (debriefing), 29 July 1968, Headquarters Fleet Marine Force, Pacific.

78. *Ibid.*

79. Kent Steen, interview with Ray W. Stubbe, January 13, 2001, Wisconsin Veterans Museum, Madison, Wisconsin.

80. Baig memo, *op. cit.*

81. *Ibid.*

82. *Ibid.*

83. *Analysis of the Khe Sanh Battle*, April 5, 1968.

84. *The Siege of Khe Sanh* (Amphibious War College, April 1983) p. 19.

85. Stubbe, *B5-T8, op. cit.*

86. Steen, interview January 13, 2001, *op. cit.*

87. Marino, *Strategic Crossroads at Khe Sanh, op. cit.*

88. Baig memo, *op. cit.*

89. *Ibid.*

90. Stubbe, *B5-T8, op. cit.*, p. 95.

91. *Ibid.* p. 11.

92. Prados and Stubbe, *Valley of Decision, op.cit.*, p.303.

Note: Despite the constant threat posed by U.S. air power, the NVA generally maintained good morale and loyalty to their fellow soldiers, so defectors were relatively rare (keeping in mind the distinction between a deserter and a defector). From 1963 through the end of 1969, only 17,000 of their soldiers defected, less than 1 percent of their forces, as opposed to 150,000 VC in that same period (Lanning, Michael & Cragg Dan, *Inside the VC and NVA: The Story of North Vietnams' Armed Forces* (Texas A&M University Press, 2008, p. 45). Thus, the odds of two defectors surrendering at the onset of the fighting at Khe Sanh, within a two-day period, whose information would prove to be so valuable to Baig and his intelligence colleagues, is indicative of the improbable misfortune that beset the NVA in executing their plan for Khe Sanh.

93. Baig memo, *op. cit.*

94. *Ibid.*

95. Huy, memoir, op. *cit.*

96. Stubbe, *B5-T8, op. cit.* p. 53

97. *Ibid.*

94. Moyers S. Shores III, *The Battle for Khe Sanh*, (History and Museums Division, Headquarters, U.S. Marine Corps, Washington, D.C., 1969).

99. Note: If the Marines had tried to push out their defensive perimeter to encompass and successfully defend that reservoir after the siege had begun, it would have been a costly, if not impossible, task, given the number of enemy soldiers and heavy weapons then surrounding the base.

100. Lownds, taped historical interview (debriefing), *op. cit.*, 29 July 1968.

101. Huy, memoir, *op. cit.*, p. 69. NOTE: General Huy seems to believe the water source was located at "the end of the runway," when, in fact, it was about midway.

102. Stubbe, *B5-T8, op. cit.*, p. 87.

103. Lien-Hang Nguyen, interview with Gregg Jones, quoted in "The Marines' Tenacious Stand," *Naval History* magazine, February 2018.

104. Huy, memoir, *op. cit.*, p. 73-75.

105. *Ibid.*

106. *Ibid.*

107. Baig interview, *op. cit.*

108. *Vietnam Weekly*, July 16, 1968.

109. *CIA Analysis of the Khe Sanh Battle, op. cit.*

110. Cecil B. Currey, interview with General Vo Nguyen Giap in Hanoi December 12, 1988, published in VIETNAM magazine April 1991, p. 22.

111. Baig memo, *op. cit.*

112. George Allen transcript of interview with Ray W. Stubbe, July 21, 2000, Wisconsin Veterans Museum, Madison, Wisconsin.

113. Baig memo, *op. cit.* Per Finkbeiner, *The Jasons, op. cit,* in November 1970, the U.S. Senate Armed Services Subcommittee held hearings on what they were now calling the "electronic battlefield." There, Colonel Lownds commented on Baig's memorandum about the use of the anti-infiltration sensor system around Khe Sanh. The legislators then repeatedly asked Colonel Lownds, and former Khe Sanh intelligence officer Major Jerry Hudson, to

specifically say whether Khe Sanh could have been successfully defended without the sensors. The officers tried to explain that since they had not defended Khe Sanh without the sensors, it was impossible to answer the question. When pressed, Colonel Lownds finally replied with the signature knack for understatement he honed speaking to reporters during the siege: "If you ask me if I would've liked to been at Khe Sanh without the sensor, I would have to say no, I wouldn't."

114. Taimur Baig, transcript of interview with Ray W. Stubbe, February 29, 2000, Wisconsin Veterans Museum, Madison, Wisconsin.

115. Letters of Juliette Baig, Wisconsin Veterans Museum. Madison, Wisconsin.

116. Baig's second Legion of Merit Award, for service June 1968 to April 1971 (awarded posthumously on November 26, 1971).

117. *Chicago Tribune,* April 20, 1971.

118. Letters of Juliette Baig, *op. cit.*

119. Lubbock Avalanche-Journal, March 8, 1968.

120. Taimur Baig interview, February 29, 2000, *op. cit.*

121. Letters of Juliette Baig, *op. cit.*

122. *Ibid.*

123. *Ibid.*

124. Timothy Castle email to author, September 28, 2016.

125. Thomas L. Ahern Jr., *Undercover Armies: CIA and Surrogate Warfare in Laos*, (Center for the Study of Intelligence, 2006) p. 396.

126. Letter to author dated January 19, 2018, from CIA Information and Privacy Coordinator Allison Fong.

127. David Douglas Duncan, *War Without Heroes*, (Harper & Rowe, New York, 1970), p. 194

128. Letters of Juliette Baig, *op. cit.*

129. Taimur Baig, interview, November 22, 2000, *op. cit.*

130. Taimur Baig, transcript of interview with Ray W. Stubbe, June 21, 2000 Wisconsin Veterans Museum, Madison, Wisconsin.

131. William Bates interview, September 22, 2016, *op. cit.*

132. Baig memo, *op. cit.*

133. J. S. Bromley, *The New Cambridge Modern History: Volume 6, The Rise of Great Britain and Russia* (London, Cambridge at the University Press, 1971) p. 751.

134. Letters of Juliette Baig, *op. cit.*

135. George Allen interview, July 21, 2000, *op. cit.*

136. Duncan, *op. cit.*, p. 194.

137. Steen interview, November 22, 2000, *op. cit.*

138. Steen letter, January 18, 2001, *op. cit.*

Made in the USA
Monee, IL
06 January 2023